Advance Praise for *Jolt*

"We hear every day of post-traumatic stress disorder. But in *Jolt*, Mark Miller explores something more extraordinary. With rich testimony from people who were able to survive and transform their worst experiences, he explores the possibility of post-traumatic growth. It is a thoughtful and rich dive into our human potential."
—*Ellen Goodman, Pulitzer Prize-winning columnist, author, and founder of The Conversation Project.*

"From the hands of a gifted writer, *Jolt* seamlessly weaves research with the moving experiences of real people who have been forced to confront their own personal tragedies—real people who have emerged from that struggle with the transformation of post-traumatic growth."
—*Lawrence G. Calhoun, Professor Emeritus, UNC Charlotte, co-author of* Post-Traumatic Growth in Clinical Practice

"Everyone knows that "bad things happen to good people." Then what? *Jolt* shows us how to grow through life's inevitable triggers and unlock the power of purpose."
—*Richard Leider, international bestselling author of* The Power of Purpose, Repacking Your Bags *and* Life Reimagined

"Perhaps the most elevating of all human capacities is the ability to draw from one's own pain and tragedy the motivation and energy to reduce the suffering of others. *Jolt* is full of illuminating and inspiring stories of this remarkable human alchemy."
—*David Bornstein, author* How to Change the World

"*Jolt* is a powerful read—I had to put the book down several times to absorb the powerful stories of trauma and resilience Mark Miller tells with nuance and insight. The combination of compelling storytelling and the judicious use of scholarly research brings alive the critical questions so many of us struggle with. What is my purpose and how can I make a difference? What is my legacy and how can I live a better life? *Jolt* will help you navigate your own journey."
—*Chris Farrell, author of* Unretirement *and* The New Frugality, *senior economics contributor,* Marketplace

"Until I finished reading this marvelous book, I failed to comprehend how some people find strength and motivation in the very darkest of times. Is some psychological phenomenon triggered? Is there a spiritual rebirth involved? Is our true destiny revealed? Through his deep, remarkable research and masterful storytelling, Mark Miller provides solid, no-nonsense answers and points the way for all of us to discover our deepest personal potentials when life seemingly falls apart."
—*Mark S. Walton, Chairman, Center for Leadership Communication and former CNN Senior Correspondent*

"For anyone who finds their world suddenly turned upside down and in-side out, Mark Miller, a renowned journalist, offers a powerful handbook to getting back on your feet. Mark's compassionate, clear narratives reflect his deep research into the topic of trauma and transformation and his passion for telling people's stories from the heart. Read this book to glean invaluable lessons of how others have marshalled strength from adversity and how you, too, can find your way to the other side of pain. The experiences of those profiled in this book cling to you and shine a light on tools you can use to chart a positive path forward after a life-changing jolt."

—*Kerry Hannon, national bestselling author, career expert and strategist*

"Miller's *Jolt* introduces us to ordinary people who are surviving and thriving—resilient—despite experiences of shocking trauma and pain. It's a hopeful read, providing compelling evidence that all of us can find strength, meaning, and purpose, even in the wake of devastating loss."

—*Paul Irving, Chairman, Center for the Future of Aging at the Milken Institute and Distinguished Scholar in Residence at the University of Southern California Davis School of Gerontology*

"In *Jolt*, Mark Miller describes inspiring stories from a wide cross-section of individuals who have undergone "post-traumatic growth" following a catastrophic or horrendous life event impacting them or members of their family. While to many these stories would seem the exception, they ring true to me albeit on a less grand scale. As a physician who spent decades caring for children (and families) facing catastrophic illness (e.g., childhood cancer, AIDS) I was always deeply impressed by how many individuals, including children, improved their own life course, or that of others, because of an unexpected and unwanted life trauma that turned their worlds upside down. Following the death of a daughter to cancer I watched her parents create a camp for children with cancer that has just celebrated its 25th anniversary. I watched one of the first attendees of that camp, then a teenager with a muscle cancer, become a physician-scientist who has dedicated his life to finding ways to detect cancer early—when it could be treated more successfully. I watched numerous children with AIDS, benefiting from the early days of discovery and treatment, become advocates for others and who are still serving as role models decades later. Miller describes some of the factors that may contribute to the resilience in these individuals including optimism balanced against reality, facing fear, spirituality, social and family support, and acceptance among others. I would add to this a willingness to forgive, whether it be offending individuals, events, or illnesses. As inspiring as these individuals are, one would hope that what is learned from *Jolt* might offer insights to help foster resilience in the large number of individuals who collapse or despair when impacted by loss or catastrophe. There are too many such individuals in our community today, and their stories also need to be a source of focus and support."

—*Philip Pizzo, M.D., Founding Director, Stanford Distinguished Careers Institute*

"Mark Miller says the people featured in *Jolt* are "blessed by an enhanced sense of clarity" and so is his fascinating book. You'll be inspired by the survivors' rebirths and come away empowered to make positive change in your own life."

—*Richard Eisenberg, Managing Editor,* Nextavenue.org

JOLT

STORIES OF

TRAUMA AND

TRANSFORMATION

**MARK
MILLER**

Post Hill
PRESS

A POST HILL PRESS BOOK
ISBN: 978-1-68261-501-0
ISBN (eBook): 978-1-68261-502-7

Post Hill Press
New York • Nashville
posthillpress.com

Published in the United States of America

TABLE OF CONTENTS

FOREWORD

We've become quite familiar with the common glossy-magazine stories of ex-presidents and ex-CEOs who go from positions of power to new glory, skipping happily from success to significance.

You know the ones: Bill Gates leaves Microsoft to dedicate his time and resources to fighting poverty and disease worldwide. Elizabeth Warren trades a tenured professorship at Harvard Law School to become a champion for the little guy in the U.S. Senate. Jimmy Carter leaves the White House to broker peace and advance human rights worldwide, while still finding time to teach Sunday school in Atlanta.

But for the rest of us, the story isn't typically one of success to significance. More often than not, our stories proceed from setback to significance.

Mark Miller sees that. A long-time journalist and keen observer, Miller finds his passion in telling stories grounded in everyday life, stories of resilience and redemption, grit and gratitude.

In these pages, Miller introduces us to people who have suffered losses—the death of a loved one, a cancer diagnosis, a layoff, or divorce. He tells their stories with compassion and grace, taking us through pain to insight and, for many, a calling that produces their most significant and meaningful work.

Americans like to believe that change happens smoothly, without ever breaking a sweat, that we can reinvent ourselves armed only with optimism and an idea. And, sure, that happens from time to time.

But as I've traveled the country these many years, I've found much more of what Miller describes—people hit by jolts of all kinds, transforming their pain into service to others. People like Liz and Steve Alderman, whose 25-year-old son was killed on 9/11. To honor his life, they dedicated theirs to bringing mental health treatment to more than 100,000 trauma victims across the globe.

The Aldermans—whom you'll meet in this book—won a Purpose Prize from Encore.org for their extraordinary work. And many other Purpose Prize winners I've come to know followed the same "jolt" trajectory, from trauma to time out to transformation.

If you're coping with tough times now, wondering what to do with so many lemons, you've come to the right place. Miller understands that people who have faced jolts have something essential to teach all of us—about what matters most in life, about values and choices, about strength and lemonade.

So instead of waiting to learn from the next jolt in your life (it will come in due time), read this book to be armed with the wisdom of others who have turned trying situations into sources of growth and greater purpose.

Read this book and be reminded that longer lives bring second chances. You have time to learn life's lessons, face some ups and downs, and redirect in a way that can bring greater contribution and meaning to us all.

Go ahead, turn the page.

Marc Freedman is founder and CEO of Encore.org and the author, most recently, of The Big Shift: Navigating the New Stage Beyond Midlife.

The Summer Day

Who made the world?
Who made the swan, and the black bear?
Who made the grasshopper?
This grasshopper, I mean—
the one who has flung herself out of the grass,
the one who is eating sugar out of my hand,
who is moving her jaws back and forth instead of up and down-
who is gazing around with her enormous and complicated eyes.
Now she lifts her pale forearms and thoroughly washes her face.
Now she snaps her wings open, and floats away.
I don't know exactly what a prayer is.
I do know how to pay attention, how to fall down
into the grass, how to kneel down in the grass,
how to be idle and blessed, how to stroll through the fields,
which is what I have been doing all day.
Tell me, what else should I have done?
Doesn't everything die at last, and too soon?
Tell me, what is it you plan to do
with your one wild and precious life?
—Mary Oliver

INTRODUCTION

JOLT: FROM TRAUMA TO TRANSFORMATION

Lucia McBath strides onto a darkened stage as huge video screens flicker behind her. The lights in Philadelphia's cavernous Wells Fargo Arena come up, and 19,000 cheering delegates to the 2016 Democratic National Convention rise to their feet. A chant begins: "Black lives matter. Black lives matter." Lucia and eight other mothers who have endured the death of children killed in clashes with law enforcement officers or from gun violence look out at the convention hall full of waving placards, cheering, and tears. The television audience is 24 million.

The convention delegates have just watched a video telling the story of a private meeting Hillary Clinton held with these mothers, and it ended with a swelling, emotional gospel lyric: "We are walking to the same place...We are walking to the pearly gates." Geneva Reed-Veal quieted down the hall and spoke about her daughter, Sandra Bland, who died in a jail cell after a traffic stop led to her arrest. Now it is Lucia's turn.

"You don't stop being a mom when your child dies," Lucia tells the convention when she gets up to speak. "You don't stop being a parent. I am still Jordan Davis's mother. His life ended the day he was shot and killed for playing loud music, but my job as his mother didn't. I still wake up every day thinking about how to parent him, how to protect him and his legacy, how to ensure his death doesn't overshadow his life."

Four years earlier, Lucia—who goes by Lucy—was a flight attendant for Delta Airlines; she had spent most of her adult life focused on being a mom, and on her work. Everything changed for her on the Friday after Thanksgiving in 2012, when her 17-year-old son, Jordan, and three other teenagers went to spend the afternoon at a mall in Jacksonville, Florida. Jordan did some shopping and stopped at a gas station to buy cigarettes before heading home to play video games. They were four African-American male teenagers in a red SUV with the sound system cranked up high; the rap music was so loud, it could be heard around the parking lot. That's what Michael David Dunn saw and heard when he pulled his sedan into the spot alongside the parked SUV. Dunn cracked open his window and told the kids to turn the music down. Jordan was in the back seat, and one of his buddies up front turned down the sound. But Jordan wasn't in the mood to accommodate. He reached into the front to jack up the sound again—and a shouting match between him and Dunn ensued. When the dispute escalated, Dunn pulled a 9mm semi-automatic weapon from his glove compartment and fired 10 shots into the SUV, killing Jordan.

Now Lucy looks out at an arena full of convention attendees. She is a natural public speaker these days and doesn't usually get nervous in front of a crowd. But the convention is something different—getting up in front of a huge audience in the arena and looking into the television cameras. She manages to pull herself together. "My whole mentality going out on stage was, I'm on a mission to save as many people as I can, and this is the opportunity to sell that to the world," she remembered later. Lucy and the other mothers received several standing ovations. "What I saw was love," she said. "We were being loved."

The women have banded together as a group called the Mothers of the Movement, and they often say that they are members of a club no one wants to join. They have suffered the worst pain any parent can imagine: the loss of a child. Trauma of some kind strikes us all sooner or later—it is universal, an unavoidable part of human experience. The loss of a loved one. A physical illness that threatens life or capacity. Divorce. Natural disaster. An earthquake. Explosions. Fires. Terror attacks. Trauma damages lives, and it can ruin them. But Lucy McBath is a member of another club too. Its members have suffered traumas that set the stage for positive growth and transformation. For these people, trauma has intensified life in ways that have made it impossible to continue as they were.

We all walk around with a self-constructed sense of our world— what has happened to us in the past, expectations for the future, who and what matters to us, and how we hope to spend our time. Traumatic events can blow these self-constructed world views to pieces. They can force people to answer piercing questions about their priorities and values. These internal struggles can inspire profound and lasting personal growth. People may become more compassionate toward the plight of others—they develop a vastly expanded sense of empathy that extends far beyond the usual tight network of concern for family, friends, and one's immediate community. Often, they pursue missions to help others or to make things right in the world. Some move into new careers and remake their worldview and personalities. Some find that their relationships grow deeper, and they may seek a stronger spiritual dimension in their lives.

I first became interested in these transformations through my work as a journalist covering retirement and aging. One of the most important themes in my work doesn't concern retirement at all, but people who have remade their careers at midlife or later. I've interviewed dozens of people who are hell-bent on changing their lives and careers to focus on work with more purpose and meaning. And over the years, I began to notice a pattern: many leap-of-faith transformations begin with unforeseen traumatic life events. I came to think of these high-voltage bolts out of the blue as jolts—painful events that stop people in their tracks and then thrust them toward positive change.

In one sense, this is a book about loss. You will meet Lucy McBath and others who have suffered the loss of children and spouses, or their health. Others have survived plane crashes, terror attacks, explosions, and tsunamis. You'll also meet people who suffered traumas less dramatic or visible from the outside. But they have all not only survived traumatic life jolts; they have been transformed by them, responding with courage, inspiration, and dogged determination. Such jolt survivors often become more self-reliant, more fearless, and bigger risk-takers.

Liz and Steve Alderman lost their 25-year-old son, Peter, in the terrorist attack on the World Trade Center on September 11, 2001. They have built a successful global nonprofit organization that builds mental health clinics in post-conflict societies around the world, training indigenous health workers and establishing trauma treatment systems. Their strategy is to improve the quality of life of survivors, to create healthier, peaceful populations, and to push mental health higher on the global health agenda.

A freak explosion and fire on the job left electrical worker Dave Schury with burns all over his body, and he almost didn't survive. Incredibly, he was back at work three months later, but the fire had changed him. As he recovered, Dave also began visiting burn victims in the hospital and working at an annual summer camp for child burn victims; later, he started a foundation that raises funds for college scholarships for young people who have suffered burns.

Marietta Jaeger was on a Montana camping trip in the summer of 1973 with her parents, husband, and their five children when horror struck: her seven-year-old daughter, Susie, was abducted during the night from a tent where she was sleeping with her sisters and brothers. A 15-month ordeal ensued as the family waited to learn Susie's fate: she had been sexually assaulted and brutally murdered by a serial killer. A self-described suburban mom and "country bumpkin with a high school education," Marietta has since devoted much of her life to fighting for abolition of the death penalty—a quest that began with what she calls a revelation of faith that led her to forgive the killer.

As a child, Hanh Meyers had always wanted to be a writer, but her family pushed her into a career in law—and in her early thirties, she was a hard-charging litigator on a fast path to partnership in a law firm. She was married and had given birth to a son, and her life path seemed clear. Then her husband, John, was diagnosed with brain cancer and passed away a year later, leaving Hanh with a one-year-old child to raise. After John's death, Hanh quit her job and has since been traveling the world with her son. She now feels that she has the courage to seek out the life she envisioned for herself as a child but hadn't previously found a way to pursue.

Andrew Revkin had a stroke that temporarily paralyzed his right hand—quite a wake-up call for a journalist who typed on a keyboard every day, as well as for a musician who relied on his hands to perform. An award-winning journalist and author who has written on science and the environment, Andrew has been writing and performing on guitar, mandolin, and banjo since the 1990s as a side gig to his journalism career, but he'd never pursued his music seriously. After the stroke, the procrastination stopped. Two years later, he released his first album of original songs, and he maintains a busy performance schedule in the New York City area.

An emotional jolt changed the life of Eva Leivas-Andino. It was the realization that years earlier, she had failed to provide the support that her son Paolo needed growing up as a closeted gay teenager—a failure that had left Paolo close to suicide on several occasions. Coming to grips with what she saw as her failures as a mother, Eva took a hard turn down a new life path far from her upbringing in a conservative Miami family of Cuban immigrants. Today, she helps run a nonprofit organization in Miami that works with teens and families on sexual orientation, gender identity issues, and suicide prevention.

These are just a few of the people you'll meet in this book who have not only experienced traumatic events but have emerged stronger for the experience. How is it that some people manage to not only survive jolts but emerge from the experience stronger in many ways? What is it like to undergo such painful, profound change? How do these transformations occur?

Psychologists have been asking some of the same questions for years. Researchers at the University of North Carolina Charlotte named the phenomenon "post-traumatic growth" in the mid-1990s; since then, post-traumatic growth has emerged as an important field of study for psychologists and social scientists alike. One of those researchers, Lawrence Calhoun, says it is important to understand that post-traumatic growth is more than mere resilience in the face of trauma. The big difference is change. "Resilience is when you get punched, stagger, and then jump right back up," he says. "Post-traumatic growth is different: When you stand back up, you are transformed."

Growth through trauma appeals to a basic human narrative: the idea of growth through suffering. The idea is present in many major world religions. Christians believe that Christ's suffering redeemed the human race. Buddhism teaches that suffering is inevitable but can be a catalyst for spiritual growth. The narrative of redemption through suffering can also be found in Judaism and Islam. The mythologist Joseph Campbell called it the monomyth, or the hero's journey—a shared, fundamental story structure in which heroes achieve great good as a result of great suffering: "A hero ventures forth from the world of common day into a region of supernatural wonder: fabulous forces are there encountered and a decisive victory is won: the hero comes back from this mysterious adventure with the power to bestow boons on his fellow man." And narratives about these heroic struggles resonate deeply in American culture—especially when there is a happy ending (think *Star Wars!*).

Of course, life is more complicated than a Hollywood movie plot. Jolt survivors have found new ways to live with a sense of balance and purpose—but that doesn't mean their pain has been vanquished. Most don't see themselves as heroic. Rather, they have simply moved forward with their lives, one step at a time, because that is the only choice they found available to them.

"I always thought if I lost a child, I wouldn't be able to stop screaming," says Liz Alderman, whose son was killed on 9/11. "But the reality is you can't keep screaming—your throat closes up; you give yourself a headache. You have two choices—either you kill yourself literally or figuratively, by crawling into bed and never getting out, or you put one foot in front of the other." Jolt survivors build new lives around the trau-matic event, and they move on—they build a new life outside of their pain. "The presence of growth doesn't lead to a commensurate reduc-tion in stress or suffering," says Calhoun. "Just because a bereaved par-ent has more compassion for others or changes careers, it doesn't mean she doesn't still miss her child and cry every night. Our best guess is that growth and distress are independent."

Growth is fairly common. Calhoun's research suggests that 30 to 90 percent of people dealing with trauma report undergoing at least some amount of personal growth as a result of the experience. The numbers are soft, Calhoun says, because much depends on how you define post-traumatic growth. "If someone is still depressed and having symptoms of post-traumatic stress disorder, but that person also says, 'I feel more free to express my emotions; I'm more compassionate; I try harder to get along with my wife'—is that post-traumatic growth? I'd say yes. People can experience it in a variety of ways."

Despite the appealing narrative of triumph over tragedy, as we'll see later in the book, growth doesn't occur for everyone who experiences a life-changing shock. In the course of researching this book, I have worried often that stories of growth—no matter how inspiring—can create even more pain for trauma victims who haven't experienced a growth rebound. I've heard this from trauma survivors like Kimina Lyall, an Australian journalist who lived through the 2004 earthquake that set off the tsunami that killed 230,000 people in 14 countries in Southeast Asia. When we spoke in 2015, Kimina's life had changed dramatically, but she didn't think of herself as someone who had experienced positive growth. "I admire your line of inquiry and think it's true, but what scares me is there is a mythology around trauma, and one of them is that you find the inner hero. I fear sometimes for the people who don't have that experience."

Calhoun and other psychologists who are leaders in the field never try to push patients to think in terms of transformational growth unless they are moving that way on their own. "We never want to inadvertently contribute to someone's burdens," Calhoun says. Rather, Calhoun and his colleague Richard Tedeschi urge clinicians to view their role in helping trauma victims to recover as one of "expert companionship" that includes openness to the possibilities of growth—without pushing it.

Who is more or less likely to experience growth following a jolt? Researchers are unsure, although some think women are more likely candidates than men, mostly because women are more open about communicating their experiences and emotions. A meta-review of research on the gender question uncovered evidence supporting a "small to moderate gender difference, with women reporting more post-traumatic growth than men." Age may be another predictor. The meta-analysis points—with some caution—to the idea that women over age 35 are more likely to report growth following trauma.

"One consistent finding for people who do experience post-traumatic growth is a set of circumstances that 'rock your world,'" Calhoun says. "It causes you to confront questions you hadn't confronted before, or see that understandings you had of the world no longer apply. People think, 'This must have happened for some reason—it doesn't make any damn sense to me, but I need to try to wrestle with it to find some meaning.'"

The connection of trauma and the search for meaning has roots in the work of Viktor E. Frankl, the Viennese neurologist and psychiatrist who invented an approach to psychotherapy centered on helping patients discover meaning in their lives. Frankl survived three years in Nazi concentration camps, where most of his family, including his wife, perished. In his seminal 1946 work, *Man's Search for Meaning*, Frankl begins with a memoir of the horrors of life in the death camps, and how he learned the importance of having a purpose in life as a means of survival. He later developed logotherapy, derived from the Greek word *logos*, or "meaning."

"We must never forget that we may also find meaning in life even when confronted with a hopeless situation, when facing a fate that cannot be changed," Frankl wrote. "For what then matters is to bear witness to the uniquely human potential at its best, which is to transform a personal tragedy into a triumph, to turn one's predicament into a human achievement. When we are no longer able to change a situation—just think of an incurable disease such as inoperable cancer—we are challenged to change ourselves."

Frankl doesn't conclude that suffering is *required* for the discovery of purpose. "I only insist that meaning is available in spite of—nay even through—suffering, provided...that the suffering is unavoidable. If it is avoidable, the meaningful thing to do is to remove its cause, for unnecessary suffering is masochistic rather than heroic. If, on the other hand, one cannot change a situation that causes his suffering, he can still choose his attitude."

The people you will meet in this book have indeed chosen their attitude, as Frankl puts it. And most say that the new purpose and meaning they have found through suffering are so valuable that they would not trade back the traumas that befell them, even if they could magically turn back the clock. The one exception, of course, is jolt survivors who have lost a child or spouse, but even these people value highly the new, purpose-driven lives they have found.

For jolt survivors, change begins when their framework for living is demolished by pain and suffering. Yet most regard that destruction as a gift. They have clarity of mind and purpose, and a heightened sense of compassion. Jolt survivors who have experienced the most dramatic transformations find themselves driven by a radically expanded sense of empathy for the plight of others and a powerful urge to help. But what lessons can others learn from their stories? How do these stories of change apply to people in less extraordinary circumstances?

What about people experiencing more everyday problems—such as dissatisfaction with work, a job loss, relationship stress, or the ill health of a family member? Those may not be "traumas" large enough to force dramatic change. But "things will happen in your life, and it doesn't have to be dramatic," says Hanh Meyers. "No matter what it is, everyone is trying to recover from something—whether it's a bad childhood, or a bad choice, or the loss of a spouse—everyone is suffering from something. You don't have to wait for a big traumatic thing to happen—you have a choice to be an active participant in your own life."

CHAPTER ONE

STRONGER, FEARLESS, AND VULNERABLE

Ordinary people sometimes find they can do extraordinary things in the wake of trauma. They often feel more self-reliant and able to handle problems, and some feel stronger and more fearless.

In June 1973, Marietta Jaeger and her husband, Bill, took their five children—three teenagers and two younger children—on what they hoped would be a once-in-a-lifetime family dream vacation. "This was going to be the trip we'd talk about for the rest of our lives," Marietta remembers. "We lived in Michigan, but we were going to go camping for a whole month in the state of Montana."

The family was packed and ready to go, and were sitting in their car in the driveway of their home in Farmington Hills, a suburb of Detroit. Marietta, a devout Catholic, wanted to say a prayer. "It just occurred to me that this was a significant time in our lives, and we probably would never do anything like this again—so I thought it would be important for us to commit that time to prayer, and to God. So we said three formal prayers and then, just spontaneously, I asked God to bless us, protect us, and keep us all safe from harm. And with that, everyone said 'amen' and we were on our way."

The family's first destination was Three Forks, Montana—Missouri Headwaters State Park. It's a tranquil spot where the Jefferson, Madison, and Gallatin Rivers come together, surrounded by bluffs, forming the headwaters of the Missouri River. The family arrived on a Friday and met up with Marietta's parents, who had driven to the campground from Arizona. "It was a great reunion with my mom and dad, and as the mother of this troop I was feeling especially blessed," Marietta recalls.

The family spent Friday afternoon and Saturday exploring the park. On Sunday, they went to church; when they returned, they had a picnic and explored some caverns. That night, Marietta went into the tent where all five of her children would be sleeping to kiss them goodnight. Her youngest, seven-year-old Susie, was the most difficult to reach because she was tucked into a sleeping bag at the back of the tent. "I had to reach over one of her sisters to kiss her, and my lips just skimmed across Susie's cheeks. And she said, 'Oh no, Mama, not like that.' She got out of her sleeping bag and crawled across her sister, and got right in front of me and threw her arms around me and gave me a great big kiss smack on my lips, and she said, 'There mama, that's the way it should be.' And then she scampered back into the sleeping bag and got ready to go to sleep."

Marietta cherishes that memory, because it was the last time she saw her daughter alive. In the morning, Marietta and Bill discovered that Susie was missing. A hole had been cut in the tent near the spot where she had slept; outside the tent on the grass were two stuffed lambs she always slept with. There was no sign of her anywhere.

The family grabbed flashlights and ran all over the campground to search for the girl. Marietta's father and Bill jumped into a car and drove to the nearest town to find the town marshal, who notified the sheriff's department and the FBI. Within half an hour, the campground was swarming with law enforcement personnel. "All we could do was sit at the picnic table and wait and watch and worry and pray," Marietta remembers.

The search went on for weeks while the family remained in Montana. The military came with tracking dogs; sheriff's deputies conducted a house-to-house search in a 25-mile radius of the campground. A helicopter flew over the area looking for evidence. The river was dragged. Volunteers who lived in the area conducted searches. The campground was scoured for evidence. "Sometimes they would find a child's sock or a pair of underpants or something like that, and I would have to sit down and look at what they found," Marietta says. "It was always very difficult, a very intense time." But nothing meaningful turned up.

After spending weeks in Montana with no trace of Susie, the family traveled home to Michigan without her. It wasn't until over a year later that they learned that Susie had been abducted by David G. Meirhofer, a 23-year-old serial killer who would confess to the murder of Susie and three others in rural Montana between 1967 and 1974. Two of the other victims were children, and authorities suspected that Meirhofer also committed other murders that weren't part of his confession. Meirhofer had cut the hole in the side of the Jaeger kids' tent, choking Susie to keep her quiet. In a confession that ended in the early-morning hours on September 29, 1974, he admitted to sexually assaulting Susie and later murdering her.

The death of a child is any parent's worst fear. And more than 40 years later, Marietta still bears the searing pain of Susie's horrific murder. But the tragedy also infused her with strength and a sense of mission that has transformed her life. Since Susie's death, Marietta has devoted herself to fighting for the abolition of the death penalty—a quest that began with what she calls a revelation of faith that led her to ask prosecutors to seek an alternative sentence of mandatory life in prison without parole for Meirhofer—a deal that he accepted in exchange for the confession of his crimes. Marietta has traveled the world giving powerful—and painful—testimony about her daughter's death and the spiritual journey that led her to forgive Susie's killer and oppose capital punishment.

At age 78, Marietta still gives at least 10 speeches a year, including 10 days touring and speaking in Italy, a country with an especially strong anti-death penalty movement. She has testified before the United Nations Commission on Human Rights in Geneva, Switzerland, attends an annual four-day fast and vigil against the death penalty at the U.S. Supreme Court—and got herself arrested there one year in an act of civil disobedience when she and other protestors disobeyed court rules by unfurling a huge banner reading "stop executions" on the steps of the court. She joins an annual two-week anti-death penalty tour sponsored by Journey of Hope, an advocacy group she co-founded in 1993. She also wrote a book about Susie's murder and her journey to forgiveness.

Before Susie's abduction and death, Marietta had been a suburban mom raising five children, a self-described "country bumpkin with a high school education." She was always resilient—her father had died of a heart attack when she was in high school, and she had to give up plans for college, instead getting a job to support her mother and three younger siblings. But Marietta never would have imagined herself in the anti-death penalty role she now plays. And when she started making speeches about her experiences and the death penalty, she was scared. When a church invited her to speak about the case just a couple of months after Meirhofer's death in 1974, she says, she arrived with "white knuckles and knees knocking—I'm telling you, I was terrified."

Yet ordinary people like Marietta sometimes find they can do extraordinary things in the wake of trauma. They often feel more self-reliant and able to handle problems, and some feel stronger and more fearless. "We commonly hear people say, 'I experience myself as a different person; I am more vulnerable than I thought but stronger than I ever imagined,'" says Lawrence Calhoun, the professor of psychology at the University of North Carolina Charlotte who helped coin the term "post-traumatic growth" and is a leading researcher in the field. Calhoun and his colleague Richard Tedeschi have written about this broader context of a new sense of self:

> Confrontation with suffering a difficulty changes people. One way in which change can happen is by making people unambiguously aware that life holds the potential for the unexpected and uncontrollable...This awareness can make people fearful and anxious...The occurrence of such bad things can also, paradoxically, lead some people to experience a positive change in the way they see themselves. A common way this positive change is described is with phrases like "I am much stronger than I ever imagined. If I am living through this I can live through just about anything." Life crisis reminds us that difficult challenges are an inevitable part of life. But in the confrontation with major crises, some persons also come to the realization that they have abilities to cope and survive, and perhaps even prevail, that they did not realize they had.

Today, Marietta's fight against the death penalty sustains her. She has told the story of Susie's abduction and murder hundreds of times to audiences around the world. She exudes a sense of resilience and emotional vulnerability, and sensitivity to the pain of others. She still cries when she talks about what her daughter endured. "I still have my wounds, even though I have forgiven," she says. "The human spirit does not want to accept death, and yet it takes time for our minds and spirits to accept the new reality of our lives. It's just a loss that is barely tolerable, if at all."

Journey of Hope includes others like Marietta—loved ones or friends of murder victims in capital cases. But over the years, the group has expanded to include death row family members and people who have been exonerated from death row. They are bound together by trauma.

When I first met Marietta, she was embarking on a two-week tour with 15 other Journey of Hope members across Texas—a state that accounts for nearly half of all executions in the United States in a typical year. The annual tour immerses Marietta in a community that has grown close over the years. "We sometimes joke that we could easily do one another's talks if we had to—we know each other so well," she says. And the opportunity to communicate and persuade is energizing.

For Marietta, the strength to forgive is grounded in her Catholic beliefs. And forgiveness has provided a pathway to restoring balance and finding peace in her life. It's not about condoning the horrible misdeeds, says Bill Pelke, co-founder of Journey of Hope and also a devout Catholic. "It's almost a selfish act, because it does more for you than the person you're forgiving. It isn't always easy to do, but it's always the right thing. In the Bible, Jesus talks about forgiveness in the Sermon on the Mount. He taught the disciples forgiveness when he died. But forgiveness wasn't for the bad guy—it was for us. You deserve it for yourself."

For Marietta, forgiving began during the criminal investigation that led to the capture of her daughter's killer. She played a key role in apprehending Meirhofer when she managed to engage him in a 90-minute phone conversation that was monitored and recorded by the FBI. One of her phone calls with Meirhofer took place after he read an interview with her that appeared in a Montana newspaper near the first anniversary of Susie's abduction. Marietta told the reporter that she'd give anything to talk to the kidnapper but feared she'd never get the chance. Meirhofer took up the challenge, calling late that night.

"It was exactly one year to the moment from when he took Susie out of our tent in Montana," Marietta recalls. "I woke up from a sound sleep to the phone ringing, and it was the kidnapper. It was clear that he was calling to get me riled up, but as I heard his voice, it was as if I was standing aside watching myself and knowing that something incredible was happening to me. All this time I'd been trying to co-operate with God and remind myself over and over that no matter how I felt about this kidnapper, in God's eyes he was just as precious as my little girl— that's the kind of God I believe in, so I had to put my money where my mouth is.

"Even though this person wasn't behaving like a son of God, he *was* a son of God—he was a member of the human family—and in a real sense my brother. So he was worthy of dignity and respect. So, as I was talking with him, a mindset of forgiveness became a reality and went from my head to my heart. To my own surprise, I felt concern and compassion for him, which he was not expecting and really took him aback. And I started asking him questions, to keep him on the line, because I knew that they were trying to trace the call.

"I wanted desperately to reach this man—and I felt he must be a very sick person—but he began to calm down and answer my questions. I asked if he had his eye on Susie beforehand or did he just choose her at random? How is it he took her? I just kept asking questions and talking to him, and I finally said, 'I've been praying for you, is there anything I can do for you?' The phone went absolutely silent—at first I thought he had hung up and I had lost my only chance. But then I could hear that he was sobbing, just sobbing. When he finally got control of himself he said, 'I wish this burden could be lifted from me.' I thought I knew what it was but couldn't get him to elaborate. So I just kept talking to him, asking him questions, and finally he begged me to hang up, but there was no way in the world I was going to disconnect myself from that phone call. Finally he said, very tearfully, 'goodbye,' and hung up. And I was just left holding the phone again."

The phone trace failed, but Meirhofer revealed enough about himself that the FBI was able to identify him through a voiceprint match. (After the FBI had zeroed in on Meirhofer as a suspect, an agent had called him and recorded his voice.) Meirhofer was arrested and charged thanks to the remarkable partnership between Marietta and the FBI. The investigation of Susie's murder marked the Bureau's first use of psychological profiling to identify suspects in an active case; before it was over, Marietta would endure a series of harrowing phone calls with Meirhofer, and several face-to-face meetings with him—monitored by the Bureau—aimed at drawing out information about Susie's fate.

Meirhofer committed suicide by hanging himself in his cell in the Gallatin County, Montana, jail, four hours after confessing to the murder of Susie and three others. "I wept when I heard the news," Marietta says. "I just held the phone saying, 'Oh no, no, no.' I don't know if David could have been healed, because he was a very sick young man. But I just really had been praying that God might give David back a normal life. But that was not to be."

Marietta had thought a great deal about capital punishment during the long ordeal waiting to learn her daughter's fate. "I knew that if he had taken Susie's life, it would be a capital case, and I knew I would have something to say about what happened when this was all over," she says.

Her emotions ran the gamut, often veering to rage and revenge. "I readily admit that initially I would have been happy to kill this man with my bare hands, but my Catholic faith, and my knowledge of psychological well-being, asserted that hate was not healthy. By the time of the closure of the case, I was convinced that my best option was to forgive."

"The families of victims have every right to a normal, valid human response of rage and hatred," Marietta says. "But to legislate that same gut-level desire for bloodthirsty revenge has the same deleterious effect on the community as it does on an individual. It degrades, dehumanizes, and debilitates us as a society."

When she began speaking in public, Marietta wasn't really ready to talk about what had happened, and she had no prior public speaking experience. "As I was grieving Susie, it just surprised me that there wasn't a pool of blood at my feet, because my heart was so broken. I had no public speaking experience at all, but it just seemed that people wanted to hear from me. And so I offered myself and had no idea what I was getting into."

As Marietta started to speak in public more often, she began to understand how her own story was affecting people who might be having trouble forgiving for much lesser wrongs done to them in their own lives. "As I heard more and more of these stories, I began to realize that was how, for me, God was redeeming Susie's suffering and death by using it as a gift for other people."

Traveling with the Journey of Hope in Texas during the fall of 2015, I watched Marietta share a pulpit at a conservative Catholic church outside

Houston with Sister Helen Prejean, the Roman Catholic nun and attorney famed for her death row ministry work. Sister Helen is the author of *Dead Man Walking* (Vintage Books), the bestselling account of her relationship with convicted Louisiana murderer Elmo Patrick Sonnier, which has been made into a well-known feature film, opera, and play. This didn't strike me as an audience with a natural disposition to agree with two passionate death penalty opponents. But they were excited nonetheless to hear Sister Helen, who brought a rock star quality to the event. And it was Marietta who electrified the congregation with her story of personal loss and transformation. "I'm a storyteller, but I have never had the experience of having a close family member murdered and had to deal with that," Sister Helen said as she introduced Marietta. "You will have a very special treat tonight, hearing from Marietta Jaeger." If public speaking still made Marietta nervous after all those years, she hid it awfully well. She gazed out at her large audience and spoke in a calm, measured voice. Tears streamed down the faces of parishioners as she spoke; when she concluded, many jumped to their feet, delivering sustained and very loud applause.

What gives Marietta the strength to relive the pain of Susie's murder all these years later? How can she bear to make herself vulnerable to audiences of strangers? "I have an experience that's unique and it serves a purpose, and this is a vehicle I use," she says. "It's not something I feel I have to do, but something that I want to do.

"It's a matter of integrity. I just feel strongly that life is sacred, and I have a story that could be persuasive. I can't tell you how often people have come up to me and said, 'I don't believe in the death penalty anymore after hearing your speech.' So, I know it's effective. And I can say that because I don't take credit for that story—I did not want that script. And I never promote myself, and I never sought to start speaking.

But I do feel this is what God wants me to do, because Susie's story becomes a gift of life for other people. It's about the sacredness of life and the importance of forgiveness."

Supporters of capital punishment often justify the practice by arguing that it delivers justice and healing to the families and friends of murder victims. Marietta's story offers a powerful counterargument. "There is no number of retaliatory deaths that will compensate me for the loss of my little girl—it wouldn't restore her to my arms. In fact, to claim that the execution of any other person, however malfunctioning, would be just retribution is to insult the immeasurable value of my little girl. To kill someone in my daughter's name is to violate and profane the goodness, sweetness, and beauty of her life. The loved ones who have been wrenched from our lives by violent crime deserve more beautiful, noble, and honorable memorials than a premeditated, barbaric, state-sanctioned killing of a chained, restrained, defenseless victim—however deserving we think they are. All it does is make another victim and another grieving family. I'd rather honor Susie's life by saying that all life is sacred and worthy of preserving."

Marietta has been consumed by the need to repeat these words ever since Susie's abduction and death. These days, she lives in a retirement community near Fort Myers, Florida. In addition to her busy travel schedule, she spends most Tuesdays visiting prisoners at a correctional facility about an hour from her home. The prison population includes murderers and sex offenders in a rehab program. "We might talk about the Scriptures or just about things going on in their lives and in mine," she says. "I don't know if it's a gift, but I don't see them as inmates or criminals. I don't see them as having done something violent—I just see them as men, and I was able to do that with David, too."

While forgiveness has been very healing for Marietta, her husband, Bill, was never able to make peace with what had happened to Susie. Marietta believes it was this inability to forgive, and pent-up rage and thirst for revenge, that later took Bill's life—he died of a massive heart attack at age 56. "Bill came from an ethnic background that said women pray, women do spiritual things, women forgive, but men take on the world. He was very stoic," Marietta says. "He didn't object to my spiritual journey, but he chose not to accompany me on it. Unfortunately, he's a good example of what happens to somebody who retains rage and hate and a desire for revenge."

Marietta found a nearly unfathomable strength in the face of heartbreaking pain and loss. But I've encountered many other jolt survivors who found unexpected strength in the face of traumas that might seem less searing, but were emotionally painful nonetheless. Consider Eva Leivas-Andino, whose jolt began when she concluded that she had failed as a mother. Her story continues with an overwhelming sense of fear and self-centered motivation—but ends with transformation born of courage. I find myself thinking about Eva's fearlessness on a rainy January day, sitting in a meeting hall behind a Presbyterian church in a comfortable palm tree-lined residential neighborhood of Miami, Florida. About 30 people have gathered here—a diverse group of high school teachers, psychologists, social workers, nurses, parents, and high school-aged children—Latino, white, black; young and old.

They are here for a daylong seminar offered by the YES Institute, a Miami nonprofit organization that provides education on sexual orientation and youth suicide prevention. (The name originally was an acronym for Youth Empowerment and Support.) The course, Gender

Continuum, "deconstructs the concept of gender as binary and offers new views expanding our ability to think about gender," according to a brochure. "This course demystifies transgender and provides education that leads to healthy responses for families and providers."

The day begins with introductions of speakers and participants. One mother, Diane, stands with her 15-year-old son, Charley, who is gay (names of all the seminar attendees have been changed to protect their privacy). "The challenge is how my son is treated in school—it's been a struggle to help him and get him into an environment that is loving and caring," she says. Another mom, Emily, describes how she adopted a daughter at age 14 who was transitioning her gender and had left home after being rejected by her birth parents. When Emily took her in, she was ready to drop out of high school; Emily is here to understand more about gender identity and her daughter's challenges. Joanne, a high school teacher from Delaware, has traveled to Miami out of concern about a "suicide cluster" that emerged at her school.

Eva is at the back of the room. A conservatively dressed older woman, she rises to speak. "I've been part of the staff here for a long, long time—I first came here 19 years ago when I was very desperate, very upset, very sad. I was the mother of four children, and I had no support, no information about what my son was going through. And I was very afraid, because what was going on in my family was not good for me, and it wasn't part of the plans I envisioned for my own future. I am so incredibly happy to see the young people here, because when my son was your age there was no place to go to help him deal with questions about his orientation, and he couldn't even come to me, because I was so scared. So he grew up dealing with it alone."

Eva just might be the person you'd least expect to find in a seminar on gender. She came to Miami in 1961 at age 17 with family members, political exiles from Cuba. After a brief stay in Florida, her family moved to Puerto Rico, where she met and married her husband, Jorge. The couple lived in California and Florida, raising two daughters and two sons. "We don't say we immigrated; we say we are political exiles," Eva says. A warm, embracing woman, she grew up in a very traditional, conservative family. Now in her early 70s, she is the YES Institute's head of donor development. She leads courses for religious communities, schools, social service agencies, hospitals, and police departments in South Florida, and has helped YES expand its training throughout Latin America.

In 1997, an emotional jolt changed Eva's life. It happened one night in New York City, where she was attending a performance of *Gross Indecency: The Three Trials of Oscar Wilde* with her son Paolo. The play, written by Moises Kaufman, focuses on the imprisonment for homosexuality of the 19th-century Irish-born author. The third trial led to a conviction and sentence of two years of hard labor. When the curtain came down, Paolo was sobbing uncontrollably. "Paolo got up and disappeared, so I went out to the lobby," says Eva. "When he came back about 10 minutes later, I could tell he'd been crying. He said to me, 'One hundred years and nothing has changed.'"

Eva already knew that Paolo, then 28, was gay. He'd revealed that eight years earlier over a meal in a restaurant, but it didn't have the effect he'd hoped for. "I wanted it to be out in the open and a point of discussion," he explains. "Instead, it became the elephant in the room." At the time, Eva recalls, "all I could think about was, 'What will I do with this? What are people going to think of me?' I was so horrified and afraid. It was all about me. When my son told me he was gay, I wasn't able to utter a word—it's difficult to describe that moment for me. It was a moment of, 'Oh my God, I've been suspecting this forever, and I wasn't wrong in thinking it. And I'm very afraid.' It was an explosion of feeling, and the first thing I am thinking is—it's a loss. I am losing what I thought he was. As a parent, I had an idea of what life would be like with my children—we're all going to live in the same neighborhood and meet for barbecues. So you have this plan, and one day something happens and your plan changes completely."

Watching the play with her son burst open the dam. Eva and Paolo went to a restaurant and ordered a bottle of wine; Paolo confessed how desperate and lonely he'd been growing up "in the closet" in their conservative-minded Cuban-American home in Miami. Paolo knew he was gay when he was 11 years old. "It was very painful to grow up living under her roof—it did a lot of psychological damage. I could always hide the fact that I was gay, but I really struggled with a lot of feelings of unworthiness, and I thought that I was less deserving because I had what I considered to be an affliction. I would hear people in my own family talking about faggots." Over the years, he considered suicide.

For Eva, Paolo's unburdening that night after the play revealed something terrible about herself. "I left this child totally alone and abandoned while he was going through this," she says. "I realized that day that I had failed my son." And that painful truth set her on a new life path. She opened up about Paolo to friends and heard from a neighbor about the YES Institute. She took a two-day communications course, then volunteered for the group. That led to her full-time work with the organization. Today she marvels at the changes she's gone through. "If none of this had happened," she says, "I'd probably be playing bridge."

"Watching her change has been the most beautiful thing," says Paolo, now 45 and an actor in Los Angeles. "It's changed the quality of our conversations. Before, I was her expert on all things gay; she would call and we'd talk about it. And later, she'd call and tell me about it—'People do this; people do that.' I'd tell her, 'Well, mom, I guess you know more than I do—I'm just one gay guy living his life, and you're on the front lines.' This has become her life's work and mission."

The YES Institute works with children, families, educators, counselors, law enforcement, and civic leaders to promote a better understanding of gender identity. At the program's core are one- and two-day workshops on communication and education. The group's suicide prevention work is focused on adult education. "The kids are fine. It's the adults who are messed up: the parents, psychologists, teachers, lawyers, doctors—everybody," Eva says. "They are afraid; they don't know what to do. These kids are hearing that gays are to be punished; gays are a mistake from God—they go to school and they are bullied and discriminated against. If we educate the adults, the environment changes. And if you do that, there is no problem—you eliminate the fear. It's so simple, but we don't get it!"

A survey by the Centers for Disease Control and Prevention in seven states and six large urban school districts from 2001 to 2009 found that the percentage of lesbian, gay, bisexual, and transgender students who were threatened or injured with a weapon on school property ranged from 12 percent to 28 percent annually. Up to 29 percent of gay and lesbian students experienced dating violence. LGBT youth also face increased risk for suicidal thoughts and behaviors, suicide attempts, and suicide. A nationally representative study of adolescents in grades 7 to 12 found that lesbian, gay, and bisexual youth were more than twice as likely to have attempted suicide as heterosexual children.

Educating people is at the heart of the YES Institute's work. The organization's courses are attended by an amazingly diverse range of people—from kids as young as 8 to men and women in their 90s, teachers, counselors, parents, physicians—YES has even trained FBI agents. But the real work takes place in the interactions between participants—unearthing the pain of being bullied, feeling ostracized, and having suicidal thoughts.

The work of YES is about breaking down fear and creating empathy for the "other." "We're afraid of things we don't know," Eva says. "It's so much easier to put you in a category—this person is gay; that person is not. You are Hispanic; I'm not. You're a man; I'm a woman. You're black; I'm white. It's so much easier for me to put you in this 'other' category because then I don't have to deal with you, because you're not like me. Rather than that, let's agree that we're in this together and that we need to work together for a common purpose. In our case, our common purpose is to protect children and youth. We can work with anybody, and education is what sets us free to do that."

Eva has heard parents say they'd rather see their child die than be gay—and that's a self-centered reaction she understands from her own experience. It's what gives her credibility with parents in crisis.

"Looking back on it, the day Paolo told me he was gay was the single most devastating moment of my life. I am Cuban, so I have to be perfect—and this was not part of perfection. I was deeply ashamed. I love my son, and I would give my life for him, but I was ashamed—deeply ashamed. I didn't worry about Paolo and what would happen to him—my concern was about me. And because I had no education, the first thing that is coming into my mind are thoughts like, 'He is going to start abusing children; he'll never marry now that he is gay or have a family or friends or a job.' This is what parents think. And when I stand in front of people and I'm real about it, I say that and it still hurts, because I need to be perfect. I did not respond to my son with generosity; I rejected him. But this is what will open doors for the other mother in front of me who is feeling exactly the same. So it's about being authentic."

That authenticity has transformed relationships across Eva's family. All of her children and her husband have attended YES seminars and have come to understand and accept Paolo. But for Eva, it has transformed her identity. "This thing was the catalyst—the first step in my realizing who I am—isn't that amazing? It wasn't really something that happened to me—my son is gay—but it opened the floodgates. If Paolo wasn't gay, would I be here? Who knows?"

Imagine that you're gradually losing your eyesight. Already, things are so bad that you can't read the newspaper or drive yourself to work. And the prognosis is bad—complete blindness within a matter of years. It might be difficult to predict how you would cope, but would you respond by picking up and moving to a new city where you know almost no one to start a new life?

Meet Kate Williams. A single mother who raised three children in Southern California, Kate was diagnosed at age 47 with pseudoxanthoma elasticum, a rare progressive disorder that affects vision. "It became difficult to discern letters on a page—it looked as though everything was melting," Kate says. By the time she turned 50, Kate no longer could drive the 15 miles from her home in Laguna Beach, California, to her job as a sales representative for a medical equipment company in Irvine. No public transportation was available in her community—she couldn't even run errands that most of us take for granted. "It wasn't just getting to work," she recalls. "I couldn't get to the grocery store or the dry cleaners without help. I was getting depressed and asking myself what I was going to do with my life."

For a while, Kate tried to keep working at her job. Friends would drive her to work and colleagues would give her a lift home. "It's a wonderful feeling to know that you have friends who will be there for you, but you could also sense that at some point I was going to feel awkward about having someone else cart me around all the time for almost everything I needed to do. In my mind, I was still behind the wheel of the car going places, but I just couldn't do it anymore. And I honestly didn't want to put a strain on the wonderful relationships that I had with people who were there to support me."

So, in 1997, at the age of 55, she took an enormous leap, deciding to leave behind her adult children, elderly parents, and siblings to move more than 400 miles north to San Francisco—a city with a great public transportation network that she could rely on to get around. And she would need to find a new job. "I wanted to make the move first, because it's hard to look for a job when you don't live in the city where you're job-hunting," she explains. "I did look into New York, Boston, Washington, D.C., and a little bit into Seattle, but I settled on San Francisco because my family was in California and I knew the city had great public transportation."

Kate could have decided to take an early retirement at that point, but she felt strongly motivated to keep working. She knew virtually no one in San Francisco, aside from a few professional colleagues and a brother living 50 miles south of the city. And she hadn't yet learned the kind of techniques that the blind need to live independently in the sighted world. She couch-surfed with several former colleagues, who would take her around on the weekends to look for an apartment. Her brother would meet up with her to pore over job classifieds in newspapers. "It was just very frightening," she says. "It was difficult getting into town for interviews—and it was before we had the internet, so applications for most jobs were still out of the classifieds that you get from the newspapers. I remember we'd sit in a coffee shop and go through the ads, and my brother would circle the ones I wanted to follow up on. It was really tough to get interviews."

Kate found a job as an executive recruiter, and she landed an apartment in the city. She remembers the feeling—it seemed as though her old life had just disappeared. "I actually was moving from a very large home, and I didn't understand the cost of living in San Francisco—I had all this furniture in storage, and I was going to be moving into a studio apartment. It was a real adjustment. I know it sounds materialistic, but it felt like I had to leave a big chunk of my previous life behind— my furniture, books, everything. And everything else was changing so fast. Everything changed—the family, the company, the job, the place I lived—it was all just completely severed," Kate remembers.

But the new experience was exciting too. She remembers one afternoon, in particular, during her first job search. "When I was looking for jobs, I would be downtown for most of my interviews—most of them were in the Financial District. And one night, it was drizzling and dark, and I was walking down Montgomery Street. I should have been using a cane, because the streetlights and curves in the sidewalk were difficult to see, but I wasn't. And there was a saxophone player on the street playing "Play Misty for Me." And the streets were kind of empty. And I just stopped in the street and thought, 'I am in this city where I'm going to live, and I can feel San Francisco.' It was the kind of thing most people wouldn't have paid much attention to, but it really helped me to identify and feel that I could be a part of the community. Just hearing him play."

Kate credits part of her success to the California Department of Rehabilitation, which referred her to a company that provided training on adaptive technology, which converts many varieties of computer software programs into ones accessed by spoken language, enabling the blind to accomplish the same tasks as sighted people. "That changed my life and gave me the ability to access my computer and once again review resumes," she says.

Trouble struck again in 2004, when she was diagnosed with cancer, requiring her to take a leave of absence from work. When she came back from her chemotherapy and radiation treatment, her vision started to nosedive fast. "But having cancer was probably the first time I was going to ask for help—up to that point I was stubborn about that. Having cancer humbled me a little bit. I felt so much support and love from my community that I didn't even know was there before."

In 2009, the company she was working for shut down. At age 67, Kate had a severe loss of vision. But she found another lifeline when a company that had provided her with adaptive technologies asked her to design an employment-training program for the blind. Within a year, the program caught the eye of the San Francisco office of the LightHouse for the Blind and Visually Impaired. The LightHouse traces its roots to the turn of the 20th century, when a group of civic-minded women started a reading room for the blind in the basement of the San Francisco public library; the group went on to pioneer concepts for employment of the blind as well as teach Braille and provide counseling.

Kate was invited to create an employment-training program for the LightHouse that included seminars, interview role-playing, and one-on-one employment consultation for people coping with new visual impairment. Mentoring is one of the most important parts of the program, and Kate plays a special role, because she relates so well to the fears her clients are experiencing.

Today, at age 74, Kate gets up early every morning—about 4:30 a.m.—and rides her stationary bike. Three days a week, she sets off on a 90-minute commute—a bus down a crowded artery to the Financial District, then a transfer to the Bay Area Rapid Transit system for a ride to Berkeley in the East Bay, where she teaches her classes. The other two days a week, she commutes to the LightHouse office in San Francisco. Kate fields phone calls from companies all over the country inquiring about her program, and she serves on an advisory panel for the city of San Francisco focused on helping to increase the hiring of disabled workers. In 2014, the organization Encore.org, which focuses on purposeful career reinvention for older people, honored her work with a Purpose Prize.

Workers with severe visual impairments are chronically under-represented in the U.S. labor market—only 31 percent of working-age Americans with visual impairments were employed in 2012. "My dream is to be able to go out and influence companies to consider hiring a more diverse, more inclusive workforce, because the doors are often closed," Kate says. "Most companies aren't aware of the technology that we have now that enables us to be such a rich resource. There was just this impression that most people have around blindness—people are afraid. No one wakes up in the morning thinking, 'I think I'll hire a blind person to do this job.' And yet it's been shown there is lowered turnover, because people are so happy to be working."

Blindness transformed Kate's career to one of social purpose, but her transformation began with that fearless step all those years ago, when she picked up and moved to San Francisco. Thinking back on it, is she surprised that she was able to take that step? "Yes," she responds quickly, "because I think that I'm seen as someone who is rather quiet, not really aggressive—I guess that would be the word—someone who often stays in the background, and isn't out in front of people and doing courageous things."

Ultimately, she says, her situation presented a set of choices. "Life is always about making choices. But when something traumatic happens, you are forced to make certain choices. I could have chosen to just sit back and stay home. I talk to a lot of blind people who are just doing that—they don't even know that they can do anything different."

And she is grateful for the changes in perception that she has experienced—like with the saxophone player on that misty evening in San Francisco. There's a heightened awareness of her environment—an appreciation of the minute-by-minute of life. "Many people have asked me if being blind improves my sense of hearing, or if I have compensated with some other sense, and that doesn't happen. You don't have brain transmitters that suddenly develop to help your hearing improve. But I can really say that my sense of appreciation and awareness has grown. You become more aware of people—maybe it's because we're not making a judgment about people based on how they dress or how they look, or what color they are. It's almost instinctive. I know that has really developed a lot more for me—I have to stop, and listen, and observe."

CHAPTER TWO

A RADICAL SENSE OF EMPATHY

Many survivors of jolts dedicate their lives to social missions, driven by a more compassionate view of the plight of others or a changed worldview. Trauma expands their sense of empathy, and that evolves into a powerful urge to help others.

Molly MacDonald pulled into the driveway of her home in Bloomfield Hills, one of the most affluent suburbs of Detroit. Married and with five young children, Molly had long before left behind a career in marketing to devote herself to her kids. "I had been home wiping butts and noses for 12 years," she says. As she got out of the car that day in 1997, she saw a notice tacked to the front door. "Where we lived, you didn't tack notes on the front door," she remembers. "It said the house was going to be auctioned off in 30 days." Molly and her husband, Harold, were very well off, with a net worth of $15 million. But Harold, an estate-planning attorney, had secretly thrown everything they had into a deal that went bad—and the couple suddenly was broke.

"It's something I want to write a novel or a screenplay about one day," she says. Her husband had become wrapped up in a fraudulent scheme to help recover assets taken from Jewish families in Europe during the Holocaust, and had lost much of their net worth pursuing the project. "He was totally taken, which is shocking, considering his intellect," Molly says.

Molly didn't know it at the time, but the foreclosure was just the start of her problems. Her life was about to enter a downward spiral that would include a divorce, a health crisis, and multiple job losses—a cascading series of shocks that would reshape her life. First came a radical reshaping of her lifestyle following the financial collapse and divorce, aimed at keeping her children fed and housed. But the roof really came crashing down eight years later when Molly received a diagnosis of breast cancer that impoverished her and brought her to the brink of homelessness. When she was at her most desperate point, barely able to feed her children, she somehow had the insight that her way back would be to help others in her situation. "I had this shift in thinking—I call it divine intervention, because I don't know what else it was. But it was this: 'I can't get help, but what if I could give help? What if I could help one woman?' This is what I really thought. 'If I can help one woman to avoid this nightmare, it makes sense of what I'm going through.'"

That insight started Molly down a path that led her to start The Pink Fund, a nonprofit organization dedicated to helping low-income women cope with the financial stress that can accompany a breast cancer diagnosis. Today, The Pink Fund has an annual budget of $1 million, and it has donated $1.5 million to women who have lost all or part of their income due to illness, to help them meet living expenses.

Many survivors of jolts dedicate their lives to social missions, driven by a more compassionate view of the plight of others or a changed worldview. Trauma expands dramatically their ability to empathize with others—it creates what social innovation expert David Bornstein calls a radical sense of empathy. "Most people describe empathy in very clear ways," Bornstein says. "They can be very loving to the people right around them, but have a different line when it comes to empathizing with 'the other'—people of a different color, class, or with different political views. Somehow, a traumatic experience can change that dramatically—they become radically empathetic."

Often, that sense of radical empathy evolves into a powerful urge to help others experiencing what the trauma survivor has experienced—a desire to make things better and set the world right. That drive is connected to an instinct to make new sense of the world, but it also is a key part of the process of making sense of trauma. Richard Leider, an executive career coach who has studied the concept of life purpose over the course of four decades, has written that finding a purpose is a universal central life force: "Purpose is the aim around which we structure our lives, a source of direction and energy. Through the lens of purpose, we are able to see ourselves—and our future—more clearly...Purpose is actively living your values, leaning toward compassion for others, and getting up in the morning to contribute value to the world."

The search for purpose, Leider writes, can be an especially powerful force when "life's inevitable breakdowns" occur. "Purpose can provide a breakthrough. Purpose can give us the will to live."

The need to make things better for others—to have a social impact—also has a healing effect. The work doesn't make trauma disappear, but it does seem to create balance—it gives people a reason to get out of bed in the morning and put one foot in front of the other. The social connections that spring up while working on a cause also are healing. "We live in community, not in isolation," Leider told me in an interview. "We're social animals, so that sense is really core to what happens to people recovering from jolts."

Dr. Judith Herman, a professor of psychiatry at Harvard Medical School best known for her work on understanding trauma and recovery, refers to this call to purpose as the "survivor mission," writing that while "there is no way to compensate for an atrocity, there is a way to transcend it, by making it a gift to others. The trauma is redeemed only when it becomes the source of a survivor mission."

Dr. Herman's research also shows that purpose-driven action provides beneficial social interaction that helps trauma victims heal. "Social action offers the survivor a source of power that draws upon her own initiative, energy and resourcefulness but that magnifies these qualities far beyond her own capacities," she writes. "It offers her an alliance with others based on cooperation and shared purpose. Participation in organized, demanding social efforts call upon the survivor's most mature and adaptive coping strategies of patience, anticipation, altruism and humor. It brings out the best in her; in return, the survivor gains the sense of connection with the best in other people."

Jolts force us to question everything and create a new life view that makes sense in the wake of trauma. Very often, jolts force us to recognize that life is finite, and that we need to think about what—if anything— we hope to leave behind that has meaning. Jolt survivors often become more reflective, but mission-driven survivors also have a passion for social justice and to leave a legacy.

Experts who study social entrepreneurship say the jolt phenomenon isn't the only motivation they see in the people they have met and studied—but it occurs often. "What I've noticed over the years is how prevalent the jolt impetus is," says Marc Freedman, founder of the Purpose Prize, a sort of MacArthur genius prize for social entrepreneurs over age 60 given annually by Encore.org (AARP took over the award program in 2016). During that time, Freedman has reviewed thousands of nominations for the prize. "It really is predominant in Encore's sphere," he says. The Encore network leans heavily toward the not-for-profit sector and social entrepreneurship—toward people like Molly who have decided to start nonprofits, or businesses, focused on the common good.

Some purpose-driven jolt survivors simply choose to change their careers. Others start for-profit enterprises or socially oriented businesses. Molly MacDonald could have taken any of those paths, but she knew there was no nonprofit group helping to meet the need she perceived. She had a strong network of wealthy Detroit businesspeople to draw upon, and had the entrepreneurial smarts and instincts to get it done.

In 2003, Molly was still riding the financial roller coaster that she had been thrown onto five years earlier that day on her driveway. It was hardly the life her parents had envisioned for her. Molly grew up in Grosse Pointe, one of Detroit's most affluent suburbs, and her parents intended for her to get a top-notch education, travel in Europe, and settle down. "I was supposed to marry the right man, have kids, play tennis, golf, and bridge, and that was about it," she says with a laugh. She wound up doing all those things, but also fell in love with journalism. She worked several jobs in the newspaper industry and did a stint in the public relations business. She married her husband in 1982 and started having children. She kept working a succession of jobs in speechwriting and marketing, but left the workforce in 1987 to focus on child rearing.

Molly's gilded suburban life came crashing down that day in 1997 when she found out that her husband had lost all of their money. The couple soon split up, and Molly was forced to scramble for a place for her and the kids to live.

"The irony was I had been waking up for quite a while from bad dreams about going broke, so in my head I had started planning exactly what I would do if it happened—and then it did," she told me. "So I executed my plan." Jewelry, furniture—just about everything she owned that wasn't necessary, she liquidated. Molly rented a house in a lower-cost neighborhood, and transferred her children from private schools into public schools.

She was 46, and her work skills were nearly a decade out of date, so she bounced through a series of sales positions for several years, ultimately landing a full-time marketing position at Ford in 2001. But the projects Molly was working on all dried up after 9/11, and the bouncing resumed. Another automotive marketing job. Selling jewelry. Yet another automotive marketing gig.

When 2003 rolled around, she was out on her own, in the middle of doing a deal to establish a woman-owned business to manufacture large banners for auto dealers. "Then I had my mammogram." At age 54, she received a diagnosis of ductal carcinoma in situ—cancer located in her milk ducts. The diagnosis was stage zero—the mildest form possible—but she was terrified. Molly gave up on the business launch. "I didn't know what my treatment protocol was going to be like; I didn't really understand cancer at that point. When you hear the word 'cancer,' you're on the treatment track and that's all you are doing," she recalls. She owned her home by that point—her mother had helped her secure a loan. But her husband's child support payments were irregular, and she was falling behind on mortgage and car payments.

By the summer of 2003, money problems had Molly in despair. She had COBRA health insurance from a former employer that she absolutely needed to keep, but it came with a $1,300 monthly premium. "The house was in foreclosure, and I was bargaining with Ford every two months not to come take my car—I was pulling out the cancer card—and they didn't take it, thankfully." During her treatment, friends and family were delivering food. "We had a lot of lasagna and not too many grocery bills. We had enough money to buy gas and pay the utilities, but I am thinking, 'We are going to join the ranks of the homeless, and my children are going to enter a cycle of poverty. How could this happen to an educated woman who came from a good family that had everything pretty easy?'"

The answer: it happens often. Plenty of households are vulnerable to this kind of cascading series of financial shocks, partly because they simply don't have enough of a financial cushion—liquid savings—to meet emergency needs. In fact, one report by the Pew Charitable Trusts found that 60 percent of U.S. households experience a financial shock over the course of a year—typically lost income due to unemployment, illness, injury, death, or a major home or vehicle repair. The financial setbacks affect people of all ages and racial groups, although shocks disproportionately affect younger and minority households; people with income below $25,000 run out of savings within a week. But even higher-income households like Molly's are affected: 35 percent of households earning more than $85,000 reported a financial shock in the past year, and they typically are able to fund themselves for just 40 days from their savings.

"I had what I call the home run to homelessness—divorce, illness, and job loss," Molly says. "I went through a financially devastating divorce, a health crisis, and I lost my job opportunity—that's it. That's how it happens for most people."

Molly's church and family members paid her COBRA premiums for a few months. Although she had remarried by this time, her husband,

Tom, had a small piano leasing business that wasn't doing well enough to meet all their expenses. When friends stopped delivering food at the end of her treatment, she didn't have any money to feed her family.

"I'm in line at the food bank—I'm the woman who once had groceries delivered, but now I'm in the line in the basement of a church for a few boxes of no-name, no-brand food. And that was humbling," Molly says. The defining moment came one Saturday afternoon outside a grocery store in Bloomfield Hills. "I had $1.60 in my pocket, and I couldn't buy a gallon of milk. A woman I knew came up to me and asked what was going on—she must have seen the look on my face. And I said, 'I can't go in there.' She took me home and just gave me all this food."

Molly has tears in her eyes as she thinks of the humiliating experience, and she confides that she often thought during that time that it would be better for her family if she died of cancer. "I had taken out a half-million-dollar life insurance policy on myself, so my family would have at least had a house—they would have been better off, that's what was going on in my head. And I didn't know how to commit suicide, but I did think about it."

But it was around that time that something clicked for Molly. Sitting in a hospital treatment room one day surrounded by other women, she had an epiphany that led her to start The Pink Fund. "It energized and empowered me. Nothing had changed in my life physically or financially. But everything changed in my head, and once that happened, it was like the horse was out of the barn. I had a path forward, found something that made sense. I didn't know how I was going to do it, but I believed it."

Molly launched the organization that evolved into The Pink Fund in October 2006. "It wasn't about me feeling important—there was a need; there was a gap," she tells me. With her marketing background, it's no surprise that she began with a clever public relations gimmick.

She was scheduled for surgery to remove her right breast and decided to first make a plaster cast of her breasts and put the cast up for auction on eBay. The plaster cast didn't sell, but *The Detroit Free Press* ran a front-page article about her that was picked up in more than two dozen other papers around the country. The Pink Fund was off to the races, but things started to really accelerate in 2011 and 2012, with several major corporate sponsors signing on. Today, funds are also raised through a national fundraiser called Dancing with the Survivors. Over the past decade, The Pink Fund has given money to hundreds of women who have lost all or part of their income due to illness so that they can pay their bills. Today, Molly is aiming to expand the fund's services to include financial literacy training and legal assistance.

Would Molly go back to her old life if a magic wand could be waved that erased her cancer and put her back into a life of privilege? "No," she says without hesitation. "I lost everything I *thought* had value, and found out what really does."

Like Molly, purpose-driven jolt survivors often experience a changed sense of values—they move away from a focus on themselves and toward a deep sense of caring for others. Material things just don't matter as much as they once did. That is how the trauma of war changed John Gallina and Dale Beatty.

John and Dale grew up in Statesville, North Carolina, a small town of about 25,000 in the western part of the state. They met for the first time when they enlisted in the state's National Guard in 1996 right out of high school, serving in hurricane relief efforts. Both come from families with long histories of military service; both of their fathers served in the same National Guard unit they had joined, and a long list of great-grandfathers, grandfathers, and uncles served in every conflict from World War I through Vietnam.

By the time of the terrorist attacks of 9/11, John was working as a custom homebuilder in Statesville, and Dale was serving full-time in his National Guard unit—he intended to make the military his career. John and Dale decided together to sign on for service in the Iraq War; both were 25 years old at the time.

Their unit was attached to the 1st Infantry Division near Bayji, Iraq. On November 15, 2004, they were on a reconnaissance mission 30 kilometers from their base when the Humvee they were riding in struck and detonated two anti-tank mines. John was behind the wheel, and Dale was in the back with two other soldiers.

John remembers driving past a large boulder on the side of the road with the words "this way to hell" painted on the side. "I had only driven a couple miles when we hit the anti-tank mine," he says. One of the explosives went off directly beneath Dale. "It flipped the vehicle and blew both our helmets off," Dale remembers. "Two other guys in the truck with us were ejected, and they had some minor injuries. I came to in about 10 seconds and looked down—I saw my right boot where my right knee should have been. I immediately recognized that I was in pain and I could see that I was hurt pretty badly." Forty-five minutes later, Dale was on a helicopter shuttling him out of the area with a morphine drip in his arm. The explosions had ripped through the armor in the floor, leaving Dale a double amputee below the knees and John with a traumatic brain injury and severe back injuries.

Dale spent a year recovering and rehabilitating at Walter Reed National Military Medical Center. Overall, he had more than 20 surgeries, and was fitted with prosthetics. He came home to Statesville in early 2006, but it was another three years before he fully regained his strength and stamina. In addition to his brain and back injuries, John suffered from head lacerations, wounds to his arms and legs, and post-traumatic stress disorder, which persisted for at least a year. He continues to grapple with some aftereffects of trauma to this day, mostly short-term memory loss.

Traumatic aftereffects of war are very common. One 2008 study by the Rand Corporation estimates that approximately 300,000 of the 1.64 million veterans of Operation Enduring Freedom and Operation Iraqi Freedom suffer from PTSD or significant depression, and 320,000 experienced a probable traumatic brain injury during deployment. An earlier study of Vietnam veterans conducted in the mid-1980s found lifetime prevalence rates of PTSD of 31 percent for men and 27 percent for women. PTSD rates among Gulf War veterans are somewhat lower.

Post-traumatic growth experiences following war aren't much different than those experienced by others, says Richard Tedeschi, who has studied post-traumatic growth in veterans. "The people who go through this transformation are ordinary people," he says. "They usually have not asked for these things to happen to them, and they are trying to make the best of surviving."

And research shows that post-traumatic growth is common among combat veterans. For example, a study co-authored by Tedeschi found that 61 percent of of aviators shot down, imprisoned, and tortured during the Vietnam War reported positive psychological benefits from their ordeals. They reported that imprisonment had "produced favorable changes in their personalities, increasing their self-confidence and teaching them to value the truly important things in life. Strikingly, the more severe their treatment, the more likely the former POWs were to report post-traumatic growth."

Even before they were injured, John and Dale had been talking about building a custom home for Dale and his family after they returned from Iraq. Those conversations took a new direction when they returned. As an amputee, Dale was going to need a home for him, his wife, and his two children that had the accessibility he needed. The community in Statesville rallied to the cause, donating their labor to build the house. Building materials were also donated, and Dale's father contributed the land.

Seeing the community come together provided the spark of an idea for John and Dale: they started asking themselves how they could replicate the model to help other veterans. That was the inspiration for the 2008 launch of Purple Heart Homes, a nonprofit that provides housing assistance to veterans. They started the organization with money from their own veterans' disability checks. The model for building Dale's house hasn't changed—volunteer labor, donated materials, and funds raised by Purple Heart. Since its founding, Dale and John have completed more than a hundred projects, mostly remodeling projects that help older veterans stay in their homes without having to consider costly alternatives—the projects include things like installing ramps, widening doorways to accommodate wheelchairs, and remodeling bathrooms. Purple Heart also operates a subsidized mortgage program that transfers equity to the owners over a 15-year period. Chapters have been started in seven states. It has received plenty of recognition— John and Dale were featured on the cover of *Time* magazine in 2011 as representatives of "the new greatest generation," and CNN honored Dale with a Hero award in 2013.

Purple Heart addresses a critical need. The U.S. has a shameful record of failing to meet the housing needs of disadvantaged veterans: on any given night, nearly 48,000 veterans are homeless. The problems that contribute to all homelessness are at work, including a shortage of affordable housing and inadequate income. But veterans also suffer disproportionately from lingering effects of PTSD, substance abuse, employment challenges, and a lack of family and social support.

John and Dale are in their late thirties now. They are on a purpose-driven mission, but the work of Purple Heart also has helped both of them to heal—and to live according to a changed set of values after their war experiences.

"Focusing on helping others, having passionate and meaningful work, has helped me improve my memory and focus," John says. He also gets an assist from technology, using his smartphone religiously to store reminders and notes. "Writing things down helps with the frustration and lets me move on, without worrying about what I don't immediately recall."

John still has frustrating challenges with aphasia, a condition caused by brain trauma that sometimes robs him of his ability to communicate. "In conversation sometimes, I'll hear and process a statement and want to add to the conversation, but if don't get the words out quickly or immediately write them down, the words and thought will be gone in just a few moments, and leave my mind blank and frustrated," he says.

Purple Heart also has helped John move away from work he could no longer stomach after Iraq: building luxury vacation homes. "Coming from Iraq—a place where kids' clothing had never seen a washing machine, they've never seen a bar of soap, there are no windows, no floors or bed frames—it was just an eye-opener to me as far as what American life is and what it allows us to have and live." He had returned to the luxury homebuilding business after the war, but found it difficult to deal with his customers. "The people I was building for were rude and very me-focused. When you spend four months building a $1.5

million home with four stories and an elevator, flooring imported from Italy—and then it's going to be a third home that they'll only use once in a while—those things just didn't seem very worthwhile or important anymore." What was important to him? "The homeless people living on the street within four blocks of that home—the disabled veterans who are crawling to their bathrooms because they can't get their wheelchairs through the door."

For Dale, one of the biggest changes has been in how he looks at other people. "I was an able-bodied soldier one minute, and the next I was disabled for the rest of my life," he tells me. "It's been a struggle to figure out how to do things differently and still have a fulfilling life. I didn't know how to drive a wheelchair until I had to be in one, or use the bathroom or the shower.

"It's put me more in tune with people who struggle with all kinds of things," he adds. "It's showed me a little more humility and helped me understand what other people might be struggling with. And I'm constantly reminded how lucky I am. We could have both been dead, but instead we have a second chance and get the ability to make a difference for other people."

There is a photo of Cindy and Craig Corrie taken on March 19, 2003, at a press conference in Washington, D.C., Cindy's eyes are downcast in the photo, but they transmit anguish and grief. Craig is looking at something off-camera, stunned and speechless. The two empty-nest, graying parents from Olympia, Washington, are outside the Cannon House Office Building, surrounded by three members of Washington state's congressional delegation. They have come to read a statement to the media:

"Our daughter Rachel, a volunteer with the International Solidarity Movement in the occupied territories, died Sunday in the Gaza Strip while courageously trying to prevent the demolition of a Palestinian home. Our loss is immense, but we are buoyed by the outpouring of support and love that we've received from around the world...We are greatly concerned for the non-violent internationals volunteering in the occupied territories. We ask that members of Congress call upon the Israeli government to cease harassment of these individuals and, specifically, to cease firing upon them when they are engaged in protecting the Palestinian water supply, protecting Palestinian homes from illegal demolitions, and retrieving bodies of murdered Palestinians for return to their families—all events Rachel witnessed...We are asking members of Congress to bring the U.S. government's attention back to the Israeli-Palestinian crisis and to recognize that the occupation of the Palestinian territories is an overwhelming and continuous act of collective violence against the Palestinian people. We ask that military aid to Israel be commensurate with its efforts to end its occupation of the Palestinian territories and to adhere to the rules of international law."

Until that day, the Corries's political activity had never gone much beyond their local school district, where they were reform advocates. Both grew up in Iowa, where they met while attending Drake University; they married shortly after graduation. Craig, an actuary, spent most of his career working in the insurance industry, while Cindy studied music education and taught flute. They weren't political or human rights activists—and certainly not at the international level. Aside from Craig's military service in Vietnam in the 1970s, neither had ever traveled outside the United States.

The Corries settled down in the Pacific Northwest soon after Craig returned from Vietnam in 1971, and they raised three children in Olympia, an idyllic, politically liberal community of 47,000 about 60 miles from Seattle. Rachel was their youngest. A beautiful child with long blonde hair, she grew up with a deep love and appreciation for the woods, mountains, and ocean of the Pacific Northwest.

Rachel attended an alternative public grade school that Cindy and Craig had helped start that emphasized getting children to understand the broader community—and to look at the entire world as part of that community. Rachel absorbed that worldview thoroughly, and she displayed extraordinary empathy and awareness of suffering around the world from a very early age.

Her political awareness was ignited by 9/11. A 22-year-old college student at Evergreen State in Olympia at the time, she was affected deeply by the terrorist attacks and wanted to understand the root causes. Her work with Olympia peace groups had connected her to the conflict between Israel and Palestine. In the summer of 2002, Palestinian advocates of nonviolent resistance issued a call for internationals to come to Palestine for a "Freedom Summer" to bear witness to human rights violations in the occupied territories, christening the initiative the International Solidarity Movement (ISM). Rachel knew Evergreen students who responded to that call. "She followed what was going on there carefully," Cindy recalls. "She was studying Arabic and tuned in to the whole thing."

Rachel went to Palestine to join ISM in January 2003, during the second intifada (uprising) against the Israeli occupation. She wasn't joining just any protest group. Although committed to nonviolent forms of protest, ISM had emerged as one of the most aggressive human rights groups working in the Palestinian territories. ISM supports the right of Palestinians to resist the Israeli occupation through nonviolent and "legitimate armed struggle," as it states on its website. ISM members take direct action, quite literally using their bodies to create obstacles for the Israeli Defense Forces in the occupied territories.

On March 16—two months after she had arrived in Palestine— Rachel was crushed to death by a bulldozer driven by soldiers in the Israel Defense Forces who were demolishing Palestinian homes in Rafah, a city and refugee camp of about 150,000 in the southern Gaza Strip.

Cindy and Craig were in Charlotte, North Carolina, when they got the news. They had moved to the city two years before, hoping to enjoy a new part of the country and to do some traveling. Craig was working for an insurance company, while Cindy was studying French at a community college, doing a lot of reading and walking every day.

Rachel's decision to join ISM was their biggest worry. Cindy and Craig knew about the Israel-Palestine conflict, but from a distance. "We were very removed from the issue until Rachel became involved," says Craig. "She was educating us before she left, sending us links to articles about the conflict, and she didn't want us to be afraid."

That day, Cindy picked up the phone: their oldest daughter, Sarah, was calling, and she was distraught. Sarah had seen the news of Rachel's death on television: Rachel had been protecting the home of Samir Nasrallah, a Palestinian pharmacist who lived with his wife and three children a few hundred yards from the Egyptian border in Rafah. Rachel and other activists had known the family well, having spent the night there and acting as human shields against the Israeli tanks and bulldozers clearing a security zone in the area.

It was a standard ISM tactic at the time for members to wear fluorescent vests and carry megaphones to block Israeli soldiers attempting to raze Palestinian homes. They would stand in the path of the Caterpillar D9-R. It's a fearsome-looking armored machine of war; drivers sit inside a tank-like cage with gun turrets protruding—a weaponized bulldozer.

Did the bulldozer's drivers see Rachel and run her over deliberately, or was it an accident? That question has never been settled, but the horrific details of Rachel's death are not disputed. Rachel's ISM colleagues who were there describe how the ground shifted as the bulldozer closed in, and how Rachel tried to climb up on top but lost her footing and disappeared under the rising earth. "She was helpless, pushed prostrate, and looked absolutely panicked, with her arms out, and the earth was piling itself over her," one friend told a journalist soon after Rachel's death. "The bulldozer continued so that the place where she fell down was directly beneath the cockpit. I think she would have been between the treads. The whole [incident] took place in about six or seven seconds."

The bulldozer had crushed Rachel, fracturing her skull, shattering her ribs, and puncturing her lungs. When Rachel's colleagues pulled her out of the rubble, blood was coming out of her mouth. She told them that her back was broken, and they thought she might survive. But she died soon after—the first American killed in Gaza in the Israel-Palestine conflict.

The Corries immediately flew to Washington, D.C., hoping to work with government officials to get permission to travel to Gaza to retrieve Rachel's body. They were in a state of disoriented shock. "I was trying to get the word out to our family, but I really had a hard time figuring out how to dial the phone," Craig remembers. "I could push a speed dial, but that was about it."

In Washington, they learned from government officials that they wouldn't be able to make the trip because the Iraq War was about to begin. That night, Cindy couldn't sleep but would drift off from time to time. "In the middle of the night I would feel jolts going through my arm that woke me up," Cindy says. "I just went to my computer and started writing, in the middle of the night, a statement about the Iraq War that I thought Rachel would want us to make."

They took the statement to a meeting with their congressman from Olympia, Brian Baird. "I told him, 'This is what Rachel was thinking about. I had to write this, and I wanted to see that it got to the offices of all the legislators in our delegation. This is what she'd want to say.'" They spent two hectic days visiting congressional offices and meeting with lawmakers. On March 19—the day before the U.S.-led coalition launched the war in Iraq—the Corries held the press conference on the steps of the Cannon House Office Building, and read their statement.

Rep. Baird and two other Washington State Democrats were present—Rep. Jim McDermott and Rep. Adam Smith. McDermott's comments that day went through Cindy like a bolt of lightning. Calling for an investigation into Rachel's death and commending her nonviolent activism, he said, "We must look at this event in the tradition of Mahatma Gandhi and Dr. Martin Luther King. A girl took action against a policy, home demolitions, that needs to have the light of day shone upon it."

"We were still in a place where we didn't know how the world would react," Cindy remembers. "So, hearing this congressman talk about Rachel in the same sentence as King and Gandhi was truly amazing."

Craig and Cindy slowly started to realize that they now had a voice that would be listened to about what was going on in Israel and Palestine, and they felt compelled to carry on their daughter's mission. "We were getting all these media requests to talk about the story and what was developing with it, and we had never done anything like that in our lives," Craig says.

Something else unexpected happened in those first days: people who read about the Corries started sending them money. "It was small amounts, and people would send it to us personally," Craig recalls. "We didn't know what to do with it...you certainly couldn't just go out and have a beer with it. And it was an amazing thing to experience, in the middle of all that exhaustion."

The Corries lived moment to moment in those early days, feeling an urgent need to take action but not sure what to do. A pivotal moment came a week after Rachel's death. Two friends of Cindy's came to Olympia for Rachel's memorial service. Craig and Cindy went to their hotel room to talk. "We sat there and looked at them and said, 'What should we do next?'" Cindy says. From those conversations emerged the idea of The Rachel Corrie Foundation for Peace and Justice, a nonprofit group the Corries founded to promote issues Rachel cared about deeply: human rights and social, economic, and environmental justice.

The foundation has sponsored events promoting peace, justice, and cultural understanding across communities. It also has supported building water purification units in Gaza, where access to clean water is a challenge. In addition, it funds fellowships and a scholarship in Rachel's name at Evergreen State for students dedicated to gaining a better understanding of the Middle East and to working to further peace in the region. Cindy serves as president of the foundation, Craig as treasurer.

Six months after Rachel's death, Cindy and Craig were able to arrange a trip to Gaza. They met with the family whose home Rachel had been trying to protect that day. "We walked out where Rachel was killed, and we looked at the land," Cindy says. "The kids took me into their bedroom, where they couldn't sleep at night because the military would come by and shoot into the house."

The Corries have pursued Rachel's case through the Israeli military justice system, diplomatic channels, and a civil lawsuit against the Israeli government seeking a symbolic $1 in damages, charging that Israel had not conducted a full, credible investigation into the case. An Israeli court rejected their suit in 2012, ruling that Rachel was responsible for her own death by placing herself in harm's way; a subsequent appeal was rejected in 2014. The ruling was criticized not only by human rights groups but by the U.S. ambassador to Israel at the time, Daniel Shapiro, who stated that the investigation was neither satisfactory nor credible.

The couple has made half a dozen trips to Gaza over the years since Rachel's death, and spent 10 months living in Israel while attending the military court investigation of her death. Meanwhile, Rachel has become a global symbol of the struggle for human rights, and especially the cause of Palestinian rights. There is a street named after her in Ramallah in the West Bank. A play about her life and tragic death (*My Name Is Rachel Corrie*) was first produced in 2005 at London's Royal Court Theatre and won the Theatregoers' Choice Awards for Best Director and Best New Play, and the actress who portrayed Rachel was honored with Best Solo Performance. The play has been translated into more than a dozen languages and has been produced all over the world. *Let Me Stand Alone: The Journals of Rachel Corrie*, a book compiled by the family based on Rachel's diary entries and emails and containing an introduction that they wrote, was published in 2008.

Although viewed as a hero in the international human rights community, in occupied Palestine and by left-leaning U.S. political groups, Rachel has been attacked—falsely—by right-wing publications and advocates for Israel, who have described her as anti-Israel, anti-Semitic, and even pro-terror. The ugliness has persisted over the years, and it is part of the ongoing pain the Corries endure.

They have traveled the world ever since Rachel's death, telling her story. They are driven to continue her work—that first year alone, they accepted 50 or 60 speaking invitations. Cindy always begins by describing Rachel's childhood in Olympia, reading from Rachel's letters from Palestine and her other writings, and recalling her evolving political awareness and the decision to go to Palestine. Craig then discusses the couple's legal battles with the Israeli courts. Their presentations include photos of Rachel growing up and a video interview she gave in Gaza just two days before her death. The Corries have made this presentation hundreds of times in the past 15 years. Their pain is visible; their strength, grace, and calm sense of purpose are inspiring.

The Corries draw strength from refusing to be consumed by anger over Rachel's death. "The first couple days following Rachel's death, I had two fears," Craig says. "One is that anger could consume and destroy us. And we really never did go there. The other fear was this: I'm not a physically strong person, but I thought I was emotionally strong. I always thought that things could happen in life that will mess up the anthill, but I could rebuild it. And I had a real fear that I would somehow survive this the same way—and I didn't want that. It is not okay that someone kills my daughter."

A therapist Craig was seeing after Rachel's death remarked at one point that he seemed to have put his life back together, that he had regained his life. "And I said, 'No—I regained someone else's life. This is not the life I had before; it is totally different.'"

The Corries feel invigorated by the people who have joined them in their work and by connecting with everyday people at events. "I do find it energizing," Cindy says. "It's so important making broader connections with people."

"Have we changed U.S. policy toward Israel?" asks Craig. "Have we changed Israeli policy toward Palestinians? No. It's pretty difficult to see that we've changed any of that, but you can control some things inside yourself. I actually interpret it a little like a teenager—it's all about me. What you can control is the impact of all these things on yourself."

The last time I talked with the Corries, it was a sparkling fall day in San Rafael, California. Cindy and Craig were wrapping up a crammed four-day speaking tour of campuses in the Bay Area. We sat on the front porch of a lovely old Victorian house overlooking a tree with leaves so red they seemed to be on fire. "You don't get better, you get stronger," Craig said. "So many families have had losses like ours, but Rachel was doing exactly what she wanted to do when she was killed—and she was telling us what we could do. We inherited from our daughter a cause and some friends, and something that we could do."

Cindy put it a little differently: "It was the worst day of our lives, and we continue to live with that. For a long time, I wondered if beauty would ever look that good again, and suddenly all the color came back into my life. I'm grateful for that, and that I can enjoy life. I look out at these beautiful red leaves and know that if all this work stopped right now, I'd be all right—there's all this life out there. I know in my head and heart that the next day will be okay."

Liz Alderman doesn't know how her son died. The last message Peter Alderman's family received from him on September 11, 2001, was an email to his sister, Jane, at 9:35 a.m., about 35 minutes after the plane hit the North Tower of the World Trade Center. "The room is filling with smoke, I'm scared," he wrote.

"My hope is that he believed the fire department was coming," Liz says. "I know he was in a very terrible place. I know there were a lot of jumpers, but I don't know if he was alive when the building fell. I have no idea what he suffered, but I know he suffered. I only hope that he didn't know he was about to die."

All that survives of Peter from that day is a photo taken that morning by a colleague at Bloomberg L.P., where he worked. Like so many who died on 9/11, Peter was at the World Trade Center that morning by happenstance—attending a conference at Windows on the World on the North Tower's 106th floor.

Liz and Stephen Alderman raised three children in the suburbs of New York City. Steve grew up in Syracuse, New York, the son of a doctor. He initially trained as a surgeon but shifted his focus to oncology during his residency. Over a 30-year career in medicine, he worked at hospitals, Columbia University, and New York University while managing a successful private practice in the suburbs. Liz was mainly a stay-at-home mom, although she taught special education to foot the bills while Steve was in medical school. Peter had finished his undergraduate degree in 1999 at American University; he was living the life of a carefree 25-year-old in New York City. "He was living with the guys, working hard but also partying hard—they had a wonderful time," his mother says. "He was living his dream, but it was an unfulfilled dream. I think Peter was standing on the threshold of his future."

In her deep grief, Liz felt a compulsion to help her son, "to do for him," as she puts it. She felt as though a limb had been amputated, but her body didn't really know it was gone. And she felt a deep need to do something positive. "It was this burning thing. I couldn't define it at the time, but it was a need to do good." Liz and Steve have always been dog owners, and one of her first responses after Peter's death was to take one of the dogs to be trained as a therapy dog. "I just needed to do something positive, for something good to come out of it," she recalls. She also wanted to learn as much as possible about what had happened. "I read everything I could get my hands on about Bin Laden, oil in Afghanistan, oil pipelines—you name it, I read it. I needed to know why this happened."

Liz was involved for a time as a volunteer working on the 9/11 memorial in lower Manhattan, but internal fights erupted over money and control, leaving a bad taste. She and Steve had started asking themselves questions about how they could create a lasting memorial to their son with a deeper sense of personal meaning. They initially weren't sure what they wanted to do to honor Peter. They were both exhausted and distracted in their grief; Liz wasn't sleeping well, and Steve had sold his medical practice. "I really wasn't paying attention to what was going on in my practice. I was having lapses in concentration, and I couldn't stand that—I'm a stickler for careful medicine," he says with a laugh.

One night about nine months after Peter's death, Liz was up late watching ABC's *Nightline* program and saw a feature about the "walking wounded"—people scarred by violence and trauma in countries where mental health services are in short supply or viewed in a negative light. The program featured an interview with Richard Mollica, the director of the Harvard Program in Refugee Trauma at Massachusetts General Hospital. Mollica talked about the emotional wounds of survivors of terrorism and mass violence in Cambodia, Cameroon, and other post-conflict societies.

"The topic just drew me in," Liz remembers. "There were three young Afghan children who were war orphans. I'm looking at these three bedraggled kids with no family, and I wanted to wrap them in my arms and bring them home with me. But as I was watching, I started to realize that we could do more than take in three children. The thought that came to me was, 'We couldn't do anything for Peter—he was killed because of terrorism—but if we could return life to people in Peter's name who had survived something like this, there was no better memorial.'"

She couldn't wait for the morning to tell Steve about her idea, and it grabbed him as well. They called their two other children to see how they felt about the idea, and a week later found themselves in Mollica's office. They had contacted him to see how they could get involved, and wound up spending a full day with him. Mollica pitched them on helping to do something that had never been done before: set up an organization that would help create mental health clinics in post-conflict societies that desperately needed services—and to do it by training local healthcare professionals immersed in local culture to do the work.

That meeting paved the way for the creation of the Peter C. Alderman Foundation in early 2003. The foundation was seeded with money from the Red Cross victims' fund, and Bloomberg had given the Aldermans one year's worth of Peter's salary, which went into the foundation too. Later, they would receive $1.4 million from the federal September 11th Victim Compensation Fund.

The Aldermans were in their early sixties, an age when many people are thinking of retirement; instead, they were starting an international nonprofit. The foundation's strategy is to improve the quality of life of survivors; create healthier, peaceful populations; and influence the political will to put mental health on the global health agenda. Although it's called a foundation, the Aldermans really run a service organization that trains health professionals to deal with the aftermath of severe psychological trauma. The intent isn't to restore happiness but simply to restore basic human function to people whose mental capacity has been damaged by severe trauma.

The scope of the problem in less-developed parts of the world is huge. One billion people worldwide experience disabling conditions, and 60 percent of those are linked strongly to mental, neurological, and substance abuse conditions. Most of the people afflicted by mental health disorders live in low- and middle-income countries, and contextual factors such as poverty, hunger, conflict, and trauma increase their vulnerability. But up to 85 percent of people with severe mental disorders don't receive treatment due to gross underfunding of programs and services. One consequence is shortened longevity: a study conducted of high-income countries found that afflicted men die 20 years earlier than men not afflicted; women, 15 years earlier. Human rights violations are another consequence: people with mental disorders often experience social exclusion, stigma, and discrimination.

While survivors of painful life jolts often respond with empathy for those who have been affected by similar pain—developing a desire to help others avoid what they have been through—the Aldermans' response was different. They reached out to remote places completely unknown to them, places that have been devastated by traumas often worse than their own family experienced, such as women being forced to witness the executions of their husbands and then being raped and driven from their homes. "If you see three of your children killed in front of your eyes, or a child held by their feet and banged against a tree until she is dead, or a husband cut to slivers with knives—we are not talking about returning to happiness but to functioning in the world," Liz says. "It ends up that if people can return to functioning, they can't help but feel better about themselves—they are able to take care of themselves and their children."

The work began with a clinic the foundation opened in 2005 in Siem Reap, Cambodia. Today, the Aldermans operate seven mental health clinics in Cambodia, Uganda, and Kenya. The foundation also hosts an annual Pan-African Conference on Psychotrauma for healthcare professionals, post-graduate students, university faculty, and staff members of mental health-related non-governmental organizations in Africa. It has provided free training to nearly a thousand mental health workers.

The work has been healing. Steve remembers his early trips to Uganda, working with professionals there: "I was still very much grieving for my son, but my chief emotion was that I was happiest when I was in Uganda with my teachers, colleagues, and friends there—we were having a good time, and we knew that we were getting things done."

Now in their mid-70s, Liz and Steve both maintain busy travel schedules—they do fundraising work in major cities across the U.S., and Steve is on the road one week every month, generally making three or four trips to countries where the foundation is active. "I learned quickly that you didn't have to be brilliant to do this work, but what you do need to do is have boots on the ground," he says. "If you don't look directly at things and just take people's word, you will fail. You can't make this stuff up sitting in Scarsdale, New York—you just have to go and look and keep your mouth shut and watch."

Steve has co-authored eight research papers focused on best practices for treating trauma victims. One irony of his late-in-life switch to working in mental health: his father—who died when Steve was just 13—was a psychologist and psychiatrist, "and I was sure that was the one thing I didn't want to be," he says. "Life is nothing without irony."

And yet, the foundation's work does draw on his lifetime of experiences over 30 years in academic medicine. Steve has spent a lifetime conducting research, teaching residents, and running his own medical practice. "In so many ways, I feel like I was training for this work my whole life," he says.

The Aldermans' transformation has taken on a life of its own. They were honored with a Presidential Citizens Medal in 2011, and a Purpose Prize in 2009 for extraordinary work as social innovators. *Barron's* magazine named them one of America's most effective small charity organizations in 2007. "It's become bigger than Peter," Liz says, "because we have helped so many people in this world, beyond our wildest dreams. It's really important in our lives—not more important than Peter, and not that he wasn't huge and wonderful, but we never thought the foundation would be this big and this successful."

That life of its own is one of the most distinctive features of the Aldermans' work. Some social entrepreneurship efforts really amount to personal projects of founders who don't appreciate the difficulty of building something sustainable, and the Aldermans would be the first to say they didn't know the challenge they were taking on when they started. It's not easy to keep a new nonprofit going: research by the Urban Institute shows that among organizations started in the United States between 1995 to 2000, only 45 percent are still a going concern; among internationally focused organizations, 63 percent have survived.

But after a decade, the Peter C. Alderman Foundation looks like a survivor, and Liz and Steve are carefully laying the groundwork to ensure that the foundation survives them. They recently replaced themselves with a new, younger executive director who has leadership experience working with organizations doing international humanitarian response and development in Asia, Africa, and Europe.

The pain hasn't gone away, though, and in some ways, the trauma seems completely fresh. "My whole sense of time has changed. To me, it seems like yesterday that he was killed," Liz says. Although she has learned to live with what happened, "I'm pretty sure when I go out in public that I won't cry unless something really crazy happens," she says.

"Everyone mourns differently, and everyone mourns alone," Liz says. "My husband desperately misses Peter. I miss him too, but my grief is not about my loss of Peter but what Peter has lost. What kills me is a beautiful sky that Peter would have appreciated and will never see. I can be watching TV and see a commercial for a new iPhone, and it hits me that he never knew what an iPhone was. He never had a wife or a family. All those things."

CHAPTER THREE

NEW PRIORITIES

While some jolt survivors are on a mission to tackle the world's problems, for others the changes are subtle and internal. Priorities shift; they rediscover values once held dear or discover new things about themselves that surprise them. Some simply take the time to savor the beauty of everyday life.

The scene isn't unusual in the Hudson Valley: a middle-aged guitar player is onstage in a small, darkened theater that holds about a hundred people. One guitar is on his lap; another guitar and a banjo are on the floor to his right. To his left is a small table holding a collection of vinyl LPs and a turntable.

The Hudson Valley, about 50 miles north of New York City, is a nerve center of American folk music. Andrew Revkin is on home turf at the Philipstown Depot Theatre, a converted railroad station tucked into the tiny hamlet of Garrison along the Metro North commuter line. An accomplished guitar player with a wiry frame, a goatee, and a folksy singing style, Andrew is performing his own songs, interspersed with tunes that he spins on the turntable, in a sort of musical autobiography. "I wanted to chart my journey in song, partly by playing some segments from songs that were meaningful to me and shaped my interest in music," he tells the crowd. But many in the audience already know Andrew's story—the room is full of old friends and other musicians who share his love of folk and blues music. There's plenty of singing along, and other musicians come up from time to time to accompany Andrew on guitar or banjo.

Andrew isn't a full-time professional musician—he's best known as an award-winning journalist and author of books on science and the environment. He reported on the environment for *The New York Times* for 15 years, and started writing about the threat of human-driven climate change in 1984, years before the topic became well understood by the public. He's been an innovator in multimedia journalism formats such as video and social media, and written three books on topics ranging from the Amazon rain forest to global warming and the Arctic. Two films have been based on his writing: *The Burning Season*, a prize-winning 1994 HBO film that draws from his biography of Chico Mendes, the slain defender of the Amazon rain forest, and *Rock Star*, a 2001 film based on *The New York Times* article Andrew wrote about a singer in a rock tribute band who went on to replace his counterpart in the real band (Judas Priest).

But Andrew also has played guitar, banjo, and mandolin since he was a kid, and he's been writing his own songs since moving to the Hudson Valley in the early 1990s. He accompanied folk music icon Pete Seeger as a sideman over the years, and played in a Hudson Valley blues-folk group called Uncle Wade from 2003 to 2011. In 2013, Andrew recorded his first album, called *A Very Fine Line*. On the Philipstown Depot stage, he swings into the title song:

It's a very fine line between winning and losing.
A very fine line between living and dying.
A very fine line between loving and leaving.
Most of your life you spend walking a very fine line.

Andrew walked his own fine line in 2011. Out for a jog on July Fourth weekend with his 20-year-old son, Daniel, he was charging up a hill on the Chimney Trail, a wooded path that culminates at a spot with a commanding view of the Hudson Highlands. Suddenly, Andrew had to stop, bend over, and put his hands on his knees. "My left eye had gone weird," he recalls. "It was like looking through a paisley curtain." Although the light in the woods had a mottled tone, Andrew couldn't blink away the paisley pattern. "My left eye was telling me that the world was paisley, but my brain was telling me, 'No it's not.'" He and his son quickly headed back down to the trailhead, but by the time they reached their car, Andrew was about one-quarter blind.

Andrew immediately went to the emergency room, where an ultrasound revealed a blockage of blood flow in his left carotid artery; the eyesight problem was an alarm bell warning of an impending stroke. He was admitted to the hospital and treated immediately, but he had a stroke that night. The next morning, his right hand was paralyzed completely and he was unable to stand up and balance. At age 55, Andrew had suffered an ischemic stroke, which blocks blood flow to the brain. It was caused by an injury to his artery, related to torquing during the jog; it's a type of stroke that can hit otherwise healthy people. For a journalist who typed on a keyboard every day, it was quite a wake-up call—but also, for a musician who relied on his hands to perform.

Andrew had never pursued his music seriously. "We all have dreams of one kind or another," he says. "I always loved music, but I was lazy about recording it. It was just something I would get to someday, when time allowed." After the stroke, the procrastination stopped. As Andrew worked to regain use of his hand, he started relearning the guitar by doing scales, and made plans to record. A little over two years later, he released *A Very Fine Line*, a collection of 10 original songs. "I wanted to memorialize songs I've written that I feel have value, as a legacy," he says. While Andrew didn't quit journalism, he's kept his music front and center since the stroke. He maintains a busy performance schedule around the New York City area, and appears on folk music radio programs from time to time. "My journalism is important, but it's not a source of joy," he says.

Andrew has an analytical mind, and a year passed before he was able to connect with the emotional side of what had happened to him. "It was like watching a movie," he says. "I had never thought of myself as a stroke candidate, but it turns out this type of stroke can hit anyone. But having that sense—'Oh, my God, I'm a stroke guy'—was really unnerving. It left me with a dark sense of running down a corridor, opening a door, and seeing a monster there—and slamming the door just in time. I got away scot-free from the biggest source of disability in America."

Indeed, nearly one of every three deaths in the U.S. each year stems from heart disease, stroke, or other cardiovascular diseases. Stroke is the fifth-largest cause of death in the U.S., killing nearly 129,000 people a year. In 2010, 33 million people worldwide had strokes.

Some jolt survivors embark on world-changing missions, but for others, the changes are subtle and more internal. Andrew's stroke forced a question about his music: if not now, when? His priorities shifted. Andrew doesn't expect to make a lot of money from record sales or performing—he's in it to satisfy his deep love of music. Other jolt survivors make changes in their lives when they find that things that once mattered—like accumulating material wealth—no longer have meaning. They rediscover values once held dear or discover new things about themselves that surprise them. An increased sense of confidence and willingness to take risks are other common responses.

Relationships with family and friends also often take on new importance. "Relationships with others change—you find out who your friends are and become much closer to them," says psychologist Lawrence Calhoun. "The event separates real friends from those who are not so. Relationships grow deeper or stronger than ever before." For some jolt survivors, the change might be no more complicated than taking the time to savor the beauty of everyday life. Calhoun notes that "it might just be that you appreciate what you have—people tell us that they appreciate simple things more."

Focusing more on his music wasn't the only aftereffect of Andrew's jolt. He also found himself taking a new approach to his work as an environmental journalist. One of Andrew's first reactions to the stroke— well before the emotional wave of the brush with death hit him—was to write about it. Even in his one-handed condition, he blogged about the stroke from the hospital, and eventually wrote a longer piece about his experience for *The New York Times*. He felt moved to help widen public understanding of stroke prevention and early warning signs.

"I'd had the rarer kind of stroke that hits younger people who are not typical stroke candidates," Andrew wrote in one essay. "Part of my drive to write about my experience was fueled by my desire to raise awareness; one tweet from the hospital was, 'Don't stress your carotid arteries if you like your brain and the things it does for you.' But my writing wasn't all selfless. Turning to journalism allowed no emotional space for absorbing the jarring reality that the white spots in my brain scan showed I was breakable—that something as basic as dexterity, let alone a long, healthy life, was no longer a given."

Treating his stroke as an intellectual puzzle—and only later facing the emotional aspects of the trauma—also contributed to a reevaluation of the approach Andrew had been taking to writing about the environment, and to his career in journalism. In one article about his evolving views on the environment, he wrote:

It occurs to me, looking back, that my approach to my stroke parallels, in a strange way, my approach to another almost incomprehensibly large challenge: that of how we face climate change. I have spent thirty years covering the growing human influence on the atmosphere and climate—how profoundly, irreversibly, and consequentially we are changing one of Earth's critical operating systems. In essence, we have been learning, as uncomfortably as we navigate puberty, that our only planet is somewhat breakable...With that mix in mind, in both making the most of a finite life and limiting regrets related to global climate change, it seems necessary to integrate two seemingly incompatible traits: urgency and patience. Since my stroke, I've struggled to balance the need to slow down with a rising sense of urgency related to the years ticking down.

Andrew isn't focused now on the numbers of climate change—how fast the planet will warm or how quickly sea levels will rise. Now, he wants to explore how human behavior makes global warming such a difficult crisis. One of his realizations: bombarding people with warnings about the problem through standard journalism paralyzes people and prevents them from taking action. Instead, he wants to focus on strategies and goals that give humanity the best chance to get to the carbon reduction numbers we need to reach in order to avoid global warming's most dangerous potential outcomes.

Andrew spent six years at Pace University, teaching communications courses on the environment. Late in 2016, he returned to journalism covering climate change for ProPublica, a nonprofit investigative news group, where he writes about how the world is adapting to a changing climate. "I was thinking about these issues before the stroke, but the stroke made me think more about the diminishing number of years I have left," he says. "We need to understand that we have great power to make the world a better place."

The jolt survivors I've talked to have endured very different traumas and growth experiences, but all are blessed by an enhanced sense of clarity: their jolts have thrown on the brakes and created a space for them to reassess their lives. For Dave Sanderson, that reassessment began on January 15, 2009, with a bang—literally—while he was in mid-air over New York City. Dave's flight had taken off from LaGuardia Airport just sixty seconds earlier, and he heard an explosion. "I had never heard anything like that on a plane before," he recalls. "I was sitting four rows behind the left wing in the window seat, and when I looked out, I could see fire coming out from under the wing."

Sanderson had flown often for his work as a software sales manager for Oracle, so he didn't panic. "My first thought was that we had lost an engine. But that can happen—I thought we'd just circle back to LaGuardia and land."

Here's what Dave didn't know: Both engines of US Airways Flight 1549 had struck a flock of geese during the aircraft's climb out of LaGuardia, and both had failed. What happened next was soon dubbed the "Miracle on the Hudson": The flight's captain, Chesley B. "Sully" Sullenberger, managed to guide his crippled airliner over the frigid Hudson River and execute an extraordinary emergency landing, saving all 155 passengers and crew members.

Sullenberger first considered turning back to LaGuardia, and then weighed landing at Teterboro Airport in New Jersey before deciding that the only option was to ditch the plane in the Hudson. Due to a lack of altitude, the plane barely made it over the George Washington Bridge. Sanderson remembers looking out of the plane and being close enough to make out the faces of people on the bridge. "That's how close we came— and that's when I knew this was more serious and it wasn't going to turn out so well." About 90 seconds before touching down, Sullenberger made his only announcement that day to passengers, instructing them to brace for impact.

Dave prayed for the captain, then he prayed that the customer he'd been visiting that day—who had become a good friend—would call his wife to tell her that he loved her. "Last, I prayed to my Lord and savior Jesus Christ—I didn't want anything between us at that moment!" Dave then reached into his briefcase for his wallet and stuffed it down his pants so that he could be identified later if he didn't make it.

The plane hit the water at 150 miles per hour and skidded along the surface for about 100 yards. Dave felt his weight snap all the way back and all the way forward in his seat. He looked out of his window and saw light, so he knew he had a chance to survive. The impact broke his seat, and water was pouring into the cabin. "It was controlled chaos. People were starting to move—it was time to get out. Luggage was floating everywhere." The aircraft had been in the air for all of six minutes, and now it was slowly sinking into the frigid Hudson River.

His first instinct was to stay on board to help make sure others got out. "I remembered my mom saying to me when I was a kid, 'If you do the right thing, then God will take care of you,'" he says. Dave was the last person off the plane.

The plane was floating near two boat terminals used by a ferry operator and another used by a tour boat operator. When Dave finally made it to the exit on the plane's right side, he saw that the wing was filled with people and the rescue boat already on the scene was full. Dave jumped into the icy water and swam to a different rescue boat. "Two people on a ferry boat reached down and pulled me up. I was so cold I couldn't feel a thing, or even think," he says. "When we reached the shore, three people greeted me—two emergency medical technicians and a guy with an American Red Cross blanket."

Dave hadn't even planned to be on Flight 1549. His day had begun with a 5:00 a.m. visit to a customer's distribution center, and when his work wrapped up early he pushed up his reservation to Flight 1549, scheduled to leave LaGuardia midafternoon, so that he could get home to Charlotte, North Carolina, in time to eat dinner with his family. Dave's job meant frequently being away from his wife, Terri, and their four children. And although Dave didn't make it home in time for dinner that day, the crash did bring him closer to his family. As a top salesperson for Oracle, he had spent years on the road two or three days a week. He also had been traveling on weekends as head of security for motivational speaker Tony Robbins. (Dave had taken Robbins's seminar fifteen years earlier and traced much of his success in sales to that decision.) The upshot of it all was that Dave had been missing out on important family time. At the time of the crash, he had two daughters in high school, another daughter in fifth grade, and a son who was a second grader.

"Before the crash, I was focused on making money for my family—I was achievement-driven," Dave says. "I was always living for the future, but a lot of the time I couldn't spend time with my kids. The crash changed my perspective. I started scheduling myself around my family instead of my job. Something like this gets you back into the present— that day, we had to deal with things as they were. Individual moments of your life matter."

Getting control of his schedule made Dave more of a daily presence in the lives of his children. Even now, with his two older daughters grown and out of the house, he is in contact with them more than he thinks he would have been absent the jolt of the crash, and he feels more comfortable now that he is a good role model for them. "They trust me much more—they bring things to me, where before they just thought I was too busy. The trust level has gone up, and they appreciate that I've shown them a pathway."

Dave changed his career too. On the Hudson that day, he had been inspired by the Red Cross, and he began to volunteer to speak at the organization's fundraisers. Then, almost five years to the day after the crash, he resigned his position at Oracle to devote himself full-time to fundraising and speaking. He's helped raise more than $7 million for the Red Cross. Today he earns a living as a motivational speaker and author. In his speeches and writing, he translates the "Miracle on the Hudson" crash into themes that go beyond that day's events, talking about lessons on topics like leadership, personal responsibility, and how to keep your head in a crisis. He also continues to raise money for the Red Cross.

Dave says the crash is what gave him the courage to take the risk with his career. "I wasn't supposed to be on that flight originally," he says. "I truly believe I was on that plane for a reason. I have a different level of confidence now," he says. "When things get tough, I go back to that day—we all pulled this off as a team, but personally, the fact that I was able to get off the plane and through that cold water, onto the boat, and survive—I tell myself, 'You know what? I'm a pretty resourceful person. I'll figure out a way through this.' My level of resourcefulness has gone up dramatically."

Dave Sanderson and Andrew Revkin experienced jolts that sharpened their focus and resolve to change. For Mark Noonan, things were different. He received a phone call one day in April 2004 that forced him to question his entire purpose in life.

A long-time executive for high-tech companies, Mark was on one of his frequent business trips to Shenzhen, China, a large free-trade zone near Hong Kong. At the time, he was director of engineering for RadiSys, a Portland, Oregon-based telecommunications equipment company that was doing an increasing amount of outsource manufacturing in Shenzhen. Mark had been on the road for three weeks; at age 52, the frequent travel was starting to wear him down.

Resting in his hotel room on that day in April, Mark was trying to check in at home with his wife, Carrie. But cellphone coverage was spotty, and he was having trouble getting through. He did manage to connect with his daughter Kristen, and asked her to check in on her mother. When Kristen called back, Mark's world collapsed around him: Carrie had been working on a decorating project at their condo when she fell off a short ladder and died from the resulting head injury. She was just 50 years old.

When Mark got the news, he "melted down on the spot," he tells me. "Probably the most terrorizing thing in my life was being in China trying to figure out how to get back," he says. "And just thinking about what might have happened if I'd been there. If I had been at home, I would have at least gotten home and seen her before she expired. She hit her head, and not knowing how bad it was, she laid down and bled to death. If someone had been there and gotten to her, there's a chance she would have survived. So I have lived with this feeling that I could have done something if I had been there."

A colleague helped Mark get his bags packed, accompanied him to the Hong Kong airport in a taxi, and helped him negotiate a flight home. "It was the middle of the day, so there were problems with time zones—there were no flights then, because they all depart early in the morning or late at night. He finally was able to fly into Vancouver, British Columbia, and get ground transportation from there back to Portland.

Carrie's death "just put a huge black hole in my life," Mark says. But it also forced him to confront his mounting career dissatisfaction. "I had been driven by securing a retirement for my wife and myself, and what we'd do in those years. When that imploded, the question was, can I go forward or not? I just lost my desire to stay in the corporate world."

Mark had started his career during the high-tech boom years of the 1970s. His first job was with Intel in Silicon Valley, and he spent much of his career with the company. "I went to Silicon Valley at the right time—you could pick whatever parking lot you wanted, and go to work for that company that day," he says with a laugh.

Things were very different in 2004 when Carrie died. Mark found himself spending most of his time downsizing operations and laying off people at his Portland company, and outsourcing work to Asia.

"They were technicians, operators, and engineers who had really good-paying jobs that provided a good standard of living for their families," he says. "We were doing three, four, five rounds of layoffs—you'd finish one and move on to the next one. I was at the point where I always kept a box of Kleenex in the conference room, because you didn't know when you were next going to bring in people who you had trained, and put them out on the dole. When Carrie died, looking at the work I was doing—spreading computer chips and motherboards around the world—lost any appeal. I was helping to have a really negative impact on communities that I'd been helping to grow for 30 years."

At the same time, Mark was working 60-hour weeks with a Black-Berry attached to his ear. "Once we started outsourcing, things got pretty crazy. We had factories in Ireland that started work around 3 a.m. my time. In China, meetings that I needed to phone into would start at 7 p.m. The financial reward was great, but a lot of the pressure wasn't fruitful. At some point, you start asking if there isn't something more in life than this."

Mark's dissatisfaction with his career accelerated after his wife's death. He worked in corporate positions for a few more years, but at age 54 he decided to embark on a search for new work, and a new purpose.

Mark and Carrie had recently returned from a trip to Mexico when she had her accident. They were empty nesters—their son and daughter were grown and out of the house—and they had been looking at ex-pat communities as possible retirement locations. "I was very motivated at that point by making money," Mark explains. "But as soon as she was gone, lots of things unraveled. You can put up with a lot of things when you feel that you're working toward a goal, but when you lose that goal, that takes a lot out of it."

Mark's focus on building wealth gave way. "The more material things suddenly weren't quite as important as the spiritual aspect of life," he says. How does he define spirituality? "To me, it means community and being a positive force in the world—helping other people more than helping yourself. That has been the biggest revelation for me."

Mark spent about six months exploring a wide range of options—at one point he even considered becoming a cook on a cruise ship. When a friend mentioned a new degree program in gerontology at a Portland community college, something clicked. "I didn't even know what gerontology was," he recalls. "But as I looked into it, I realized that aging was a growth industry—sort of like high tech was back in the '70s. You could see the age tsunami coming, and how our society is very ill-prepared for it. I never thought I'd make a lot of money doing it, but that wasn't really the objective." With a sufficient financial cushion to go back to school, Mark earned an associate degree in the program and followed that up with several internships at local nonprofits. Eventually, he accepted a position as outreach director at Elders in Action, a local nonprofit advocacy group.

Now in his mid-60s, Mark maintains a flexible schedule, sometimes working from home and balancing work and personal priorities. His technology skills have been a plus—he set up the group's social media presence and manages its email and contact databases. But mainly, he's out in the community. "I'm a community-engagement guy—lining up events and making sure we have a presence at community gatherings," he says. "We train our volunteers on how to help folks who call us with housing problems, or maybe healthcare issues, or they've been victimized by scams or frauds or elder abuse. We give them a real person to help them work through it."

Mark's experiences have given him a special ability to connect with people going through their own tough transitions. "It's being able to sit down and say, 'There are often these things that will transition you to something better,' and to be able to talk about alternatives and options—how people can use their passion to actually make a change in their lives."

Mark thinks if tragedy had not struck, he would probably still be stuck in his old life despite his growing unhappiness—he simply wouldn't have been motivated to make a change like this on his own. "Lots of different tragedies happen that make people go out and reassess their lives. Mine, unfortunately, had to do with losing my wife, which I'll never get over. But it was a catalyst."

Mark, who has not remarried since Carrie's death, also thinks his jolt makes it easier for him to understand what other people are going through when they come to Elders in Action for help. "These things come along and people get paralyzed by them," he says. "It takes some effort, and a lot of will, but there is a way back if you spend some time pushing yourself."

Most important, Mark's jolt uncovered questions he never expected to be asking himself. "For me this was a rebirth moment," he says. "It left me thinking, 'Why am I doing this? What's my purpose in life?'"

Hanh Meyers might not describe her jolt as a "rebirth" the way that Mark Noonan does. But she allows that she is doing things these days that "are very unlike me." Hanh, a 36-year-old attorney, has always been a list maker. "I usually have a Plan A, Plan B, and Plan C," she says. Once a hard-charging commercial litigator with ambitious plans for her career in law, she now finds herself doing much more improvising. "It's unsettling to me, and disconcerting," she says with a laugh. "I don't have a particular goal that I'm trying to achieve anymore. I'm trusting the universe to lead me where I need to go. Or, trusting myself."

Several years ago, the universe knocked her down hard, sending her on a journey that forced her to question her sense of identity and reevaluate her life goals. One night in March 2013, she was putting her infant son, Liam, to bed when she found her husband, John, on the floor of their Chicago apartment. He seemed to be having a seizure, and Hanh called 911 immediately. A mass was found in John's brain, and he underwent emergency surgery a few days later. The diagnosis was glioblastoma, a highly malignant type of brain tumor with a median survival time of about 15 months. John died a little more than a year later at age 42, just after their sixth wedding anniversary. Hanh was 34 years old; the couple had celebrated Liam's first birthday two months before.

John and Hanh met while both were studying for their law degrees at Loyola University in Chicago; both worked on the school's *International Law Review*. They couldn't have come from more different backgrounds: John grew up in central Illinois, while Hanh left her native Cambodia when she was just two years old with her family, who were fleeing the genocidal reign of the Khmer Rouge, arriving in the United States as a refugee. She was separated from her parents during the escape while crossing the border into Thailand. Relatives have told Hanh that the Khmer Rouge spotted them about 500 feet from the border and gave chase; her mother fell and twisted her ankle, and her father stopped to help, giving Hanh to her aunt and telling them to run across the border and wait for them. Her parents never crossed.

Hanh was raised by her aunt in Tacoma, Washington, and later in northern Virginia. They were not close, and childhood wasn't a happy time for Hanh. As a child, she read all the books she could get her hands on, and spent a lot of time writing in her journal. "Marrying John, and then having Liam, I finally felt I had the family I wanted," she says. "I couldn't have the family I wanted with loving parents, but with John, that was the start of creating the family I wanted to have."

A career in law wasn't so much an affirmative choice for Hanh as a pathway she felt pushed into by her family. "I grew up in a very traditional Asian household," she says. "As a child, I was told I could only grow up to be a doctor or a lawyer." John had earned an MBA before enrolling in law school, and after law school he worked for the finance division of an automaker and then as a vice president for a Chicago bank. He was working on a degree in computer science when he fell ill. Hanh was working at a small law firm handling commercial litigation. "I remember thinking, 'Here I am, having to grieve the death of my husband, because he is surely going to die,' and having to plan that and live through this while I should be celebrating the life of my son and planning for his life, and all the dreams that encompassed. That kicked off a 15-month journey of life and death. I was experiencing the dichotomy of it so acutely every minute."

The couple loved to travel, taking one international trip every year, and now they decided to squeeze in as much travel as John's health would allow, spending money they had saved for a down payment on a house. "I said, 'We're not going to have this house together, so let's go.'" Hanh quit her job in February 2014, and they left for Norway to see the northern lights. Hanh said to John, "I don't know how much time we're going to have together—why don't we try? You could have five years left, or a year." Liam, who was 11 months old at the time, traveled with them.

John had a brain scan just before they left, and his doctors approved the trip, but the travel was difficult. "You fool yourself into thinking that things are normal, but they aren't," Hanh says. The cancer already was affecting the cognitive function of John's brain; the business road warrior now couldn't handle his own travel papers or passport, or even carry a suitcase. But Hanh says he was able to enjoy the trip and take photos, and the couple was glad to have been able to make at least one family trip with Liam.

Hanh and John had planned a cruise in Alaska that they didn't get to take. John passed away at the end of June 2014; his funeral was held on Liam's 16-month birthday. Hanh was now a widow, a single parent, and a caregiver to boot. John had been an only child; his parents, who still lived in central Illinois, were reclusive and dependent on Hanh after their son's death. His mother passed away four months after John; his father was still alive but had Alzheimer's disease, and Hanh took over responsibility for his care, moving him into an assisted-living facility and shouldering the burden of emptying out her in-laws' house. "I thought I was the butt of the biggest cosmic joke ever. Here I thought I was supposed to be on this trajectory of working at a law firm, getting a house in the suburbs, and having all these kids. Instead, I hadn't even turned 35—I was a widow, a single parent, and a caregiver to an elderly parent who was not my own," Hanh says. Closing and selling her in-laws' home was an out-of-body experience—going through old family photos of people Hanh didn't know, and deciding what to keep and what to toss. "John's mom kept everything, right down to the Valentine's Day card he gave her when he was in first grade."

After John's death, Hanh often heard people say that Liam was the legacy he had left, but she wasn't comfortable with that. "John didn't give me Liam—we decided to do that together," she tells me. She had a different idea about what John had left her. "I had a fear of dying—when you see it around the corner and taste it, you have a fear of mortality—and I wanted to see the world before I died." He also had left her the financial means to explore what she wanted from her life; he had bought life insurance after Liam's birth, before his diagnosis.

John's death, and Liam's birth, gave Hanh the courage to stand up for the life she envisioned for herself but hadn't been able to pursue for fear of failure. Hanh cast off the identity that was imposed on her while she was growing up. Looking back, Hahn says the way she had made decisions was "very rigid."

"First, I decided to be a lawyer, not a doctor. If I'm going to be a lawyer, I should go into litigation because that's real law, right? The path was laid out, and it seemed nice and safe: go to law school, join a firm, and go up the ladder. I enjoyed it enough—the research, the writing, representing people, and talking with other professional colleagues."

In the wake of John's death, Hanh felt something was missing: a sense of control over the decisions she was making. Rather than go back to work, she opted to travel the world with Liam. They have spent time in northern Europe, the Baltics, Greece, Croatia, Italy, India, Nepal, Singapore, Indonesia, Australia, New Zealand, and Japan. "It's been incredible spending so much time with my son," Hanh told me when I caught up with her mid-trip in Paris. "I didn't realize that he talked so much or talked all the time—traveling with a toddler, and meeting the needs of a three-year-old, presents its own challenges."

Their typical travel day starts with breakfast and an outing—perhaps a boat ride and a little sightseeing. Then lunch and a nap, followed by a playground visit. She doesn't expect to return to her work as an attorney. "I think I'm done with the law. I just don't think I have the passion for it," she says. "I have a great deal of respect for litigators—it's really difficult work—but I don't want to spend my life being in contention with other people. I want to make sure that I find a way to spend my days productively, but with much more of a sense of fulfillment."

She also won't be returning to her home in Chicago. Before leaving town with Liam, she rented out her Chicago condominium and put all her possessions in storage. "Liam said to me before we left, 'Mama, we're traveling around the world to find a new home.'" She thinks she might return to France to live—she studied there in high school and college, and speaks French well.

Before leaving on her trip with Liam, Hanh also took a course in creative writing, and says she is "still working on that."

Complacency is her biggest fear now. "I fear making choices that seem reasonable and safe without really thinking whether it's what I want, and wind up making choices that have little heart. I'm still figuring out where I'm going and what this is all leading to. It's unsettling and scary, but if I don't take the time, I feel like I am wasting John's death."

Hanh no longer thinks of herself as someone who needs to know the life path ahead of her. She still is not in full control—but she is comfortable with that. "There is comfort in knowing what is in front of you and seeing a particular future—thinking that you'll go to work, raise a family, save for retirement, and visit with your grandchildren. I always knew I wanted to try my hand at writing, but why give up the comfort of a job and a 401(k) plan to do something where I might utterly fail? Now, I can't see a future, and that is unsettling. But I also feel willing to accept life on whatever terms it is offering me." She feels that her identity is changing, "but I just don't know what it is yet. I'm floating and searching."

CHAPTER FOUR

THE PROCESS OF CHANGE

For most jolt survivors, transformation doesn't happen overnight. It takes time—varying amounts of it. But change always begins with an event that makes the ground shift—something that causes people to consider questions they have not confronted before or to change the way they perceive the world.

Dave Schury heard a roaring sound behind him. He knew what to expect next: a flash of light and searing flames that would envelop his body.

Dave repaired 12,000-volt electrical lines for a living as a high-voltage troubleshooter at Commonwealth Edison, the Chicago utility company. On April 13, 2000, he was standing in front of a switching station at a public housing project on Chicago's South Side. His repair crew partner had just finished switching back on a repaired cable that provided power to three high-rise apartment buildings in the Robert Taylor homes. Dave stepped over to the side of the large metal box, about the size of three large refrigerators sitting side by side. "I was writing in the logbook what we did, the date, and who did the work. I was going to put the log back in the compartment where it's stored—that's all I had to do. I bent down to replace it when I heard a big roar and a boom. I knew what was coming, and something terrible was going to happen, because I've heard it so many times before—it was just never right there in front of me."

Workers who repair these lines always face the risk of electrical shock or electrocution. Age 35 at the time, Dave was an experienced electrical worker with a great safety record—he had been with the company since he was just 20 years old. That morning, he was the victim of a freak accident: a rat had gotten inside the switch box and short-circuited a 7,200-volt bus bar. "It was crawling around in there and became a little piece of circuit. Instead of power flowing through the circuit, it took the shorter path through the ground," Dave explains.

When electrical current leaves its intended path and travels through the air from one conductor to another, or to the ground, it creates an arc flash—a huge ball of fire. Arc flashes are short in duration—after just a few seconds, a circuit breaker shuts off power. But arc flashes get as hot as 35,000 degrees Fahrenheit, and the blast pressure can exceed 2,000 pounds per square foot. Flying objects like molten metal can become embedded in the body of anyone unfortunate enough to be nearby.

When repair crews do jobs like this, they wear protective gear, and Dave was wearing a fire-resistant pair of jeans and shirt, a hard hat, and safety glasses. The fireball came straight at him as he bent down to replace the log. The force of the explosion blew Dave eight feet back to his truck. He could see molten metal splattered all over the truck. Dave's protective clothing and safety glasses protected his skin and eyes from the metal, but his fire-resistant shirt was gone. His T-shirt underneath and hardhat were blackened by the fire, and the hat's plastic liner had melted to his head.

Dave knew he had been badly hurt. "I knew I'd been burned. My whole life, I knew this happens, and the only place I never wanted to get burned was my face. I always thought, 'Just don't let me get burned on my face.' I walked over to my truck and looked in the rear-view mirror, and I could see the skin hanging off my face." Dave initially thought his partner—who was on the ground—had been more badly injured; however, he sustained only minor burns on his leg and was released from the hospital that same day. Dave was able to call his dispatcher and boss, and then he called the medical office where his wife, Michele, worked. Dave knew from other arc flashes that he was in bad shape, and he knew what was coming.

"I knew from other accidents where guys got hurt that I would be in a coma before they would even get to the hospital. I knew I was in bad shape. I just wanted to tell her I loved her and the girls. I just wanted to let them know...reassure them and [let them] hear my voice. And after I talked to her it was like, 'Okay—I'm done.'"

Dave had experienced second-degree burns on 30 percent of his body. He spent eight days in an induced coma at the burn unit of the Cook County hospital on a ventilator. He doesn't remember much of those days, because he was on a painkiller with an amnesia side effect. His face was dark red, as though he had a very bad sunburn. Nurses would scrub his face twice a day, one side at a time because the pain was so intense. Doctors weren't sure he would survive.

Dave did make it, returning home two weeks later, and gradually recovered. Only three months later, he was back at work, and he even managed to face down his fear of another explosion, getting back to the outdoor line work that he loved. But the arc flash fire began a process of change in the lives both of Dave and Michele. Sixteen years later, the former hardhat electrical worker runs From Tragedy to Triumph, a foundation that raises money to fund scholarships for burn survivors. He also spends many hours every year providing support to burn victims during and after their hospitalization through a program called Phoenix SOAR (Survivors Offering Assistance in Recovery).

But for Dave, like many jolt survivors, the transformation didn't happen overnight. "You don't just wake up one morning and say, 'I'm going to save the world,'" he says. What is the nature of recovery and change for people who experience post-traumatic growth? What influences them, and what does change look like from their perspective?

Some stories of post-traumatic growth occur on a grand scale and with a transformation that occurs suddenly, sometimes overnight, seemingly changing the entire direction of the survivors' lives. More often, change occurs slowly, as a result of many small, halting steps. These survivors simply put one foot in front of the other.

For most jolt survivors, their social environment also plays a critical role in shaping the path to recovery and growth. That includes the interaction and support of the people closest to them—spouses, family members, and friends. And just as important is cultural context, the set of values and beliefs that govern a jolt survivor's sense of right and wrong and how to act in the world. Lawrence Calhoun and Richard Tedeschi, pioneers in the study of post-traumatic growth at the University of North Carolina at Charlotte, call these influences "primary reference groups"—family members, friends, religious organizations, neighbors, or professional peers.

Dave Schury didn't rely on others much before the burns. He's the strong, silent type—a stocky man with close-cropped hair and a generous grin. "He's not one to get support from anyone," his wife, Michele, says with a smile. But he saw a psychologist during his recovery, which helped him open up and work through the trauma. When the accident occurred, Dave and Michele had just celebrated their tenth wedding anniversary and had a very solid marriage. They both worried that the accident might hurt their relationship, but important new bonds surfaced instead. "On the days when you are down, you hope the other person is there to help pick you up," Dave says. "We had a good life together, and I didn't want to lose that. Michele was there to carry the entire load, but after I started getting better, I knew she was going to need the support, because she was going to need to let it all out."

Dave retired from Commonwealth Edison in 2014, and if not for the accident, he tells me, he'd probably be enjoying his two grandchildren and playing a lot of golf right now. Instead, he started down a new path.

The first step was burn camp.

The Illinois Fire Safety Alliance has run Camp "I Am Me" since 1991. Held at a YMCA camp on the outskirts of Chicago's suburbs, it brings together 80 kids who have suffered burns, at no charge, every year. Camp starts the Sunday of Father's Day weekend and runs for six days. The ages range from eight to sixteen; some campers' burns are so recent that they're still in bandages; others have recovered physically but still struggle with emotional problems. Fifty counselors and a medical staff look after the campers' needs. Other than that, it's just a regular summer camp, with activities like swimming, canoeing, fishing, crafts, and a climbing wall with high ropes.

Dave heard about burn camp in the first year of his recovery, during a visit with the Chicago Fire Department paramedics who had taken care of him on the scene of the explosion. "A good friend of mine who was a fireman mentioned it to me," Dave remembers. "He said, 'You know, you might just want to check into this—a lot of firemen go there and volunteer their time as counselors.'"

Dave wanted to apply to be a counselor but learned that he had just a few days to meet the application deadline for the next camp; the requirements included a physical exam. "It's not something I'll ever forget," says Mary Werderitch, the fire safety group's executive director. "He filled out that application the minute he got it and brought it to my house—and I live a good hour away. No one had ever done that before."

Dave went to burn camp that year as a counselor. It wasn't part of some grand plan he had developed for rehabbing his life. "You really don't know what your future is to be at that point, so you just grasp at everything to see where it can lead," Michele says. "You get in this mode where you just keep going—it's not like you know the direction, because everything is so emotional and raw. You just keep going."

Dave thought he was going to provide help and support to the children but was surprised to see almost immediately that camp was a two-way street. He was still wearing pressure sleeves that covered the burns on his arms. "I was talking with a 10-year-old kid who told me, 'You don't need to cover up your burns, because we're all the same here at camp.' I wasn't hiding them, but here he was thinking that I was afraid to show other people my scars, so he was trying to help me. I was 45 years old, and here was this 10-year-old boy trying to console me as an adult."

He adds, "I didn't know what to expect. I was excited about going, but emotionally it was very hard to handle. It was sunglasses all the time, I was crying so much."

Dave was hooked—he knew he'd be a burn camp counselor for life. His daughter Chrisele puts it this way: "The kids at camp made him who he is today." But he came away from camp knowing he wanted to do more, and one thing led to another. It was at camp that he first heard about Phoenix SOAR, a national organization based in Grand Rapids, Michigan, that provides peer support, education, and advocacy for burn survivors and their families. Loyola University Medical Center had recently launched SOAR at its burn unit in the Chicago area.

SOAR's purpose is simple: to connect burn survivors with a compassionate community of other people who know what they are going through, because they've been there. Volunteers provide one-on-one peer support to survivors while they're still in the hospital. SOAR has trained more than 700 burn survivors to provide peer support in 64 burn centers around the country. Survivors can include anyone affected by the injuries—the survivors themselves, their spouses, siblings, or other family members.

The key to SOAR is providing a peer connection to survivors early in their process of recovery. "It's not medical advice—it's about role modeling," says Amy Acton, the executive director of SOAR. "We teach active listening, and how to answer questions about the emotional aspects of recovery—how you got through the experience and to put forward an image of hope—you recovered, maybe I can too. And the survivor has different questions for someone who has been there than they would have for a nurse or doctor."

"We couldn't fathom another family going through what we went through without support," Michele says. They went through training and began visiting patients in the fall of 2002. Over the next decade, they both would visit with patients and their spouses in the hospital and provide support over the phone and by attending every-other-month support groups at the hospital.

Dave has supported electrical workers who've been in accidents, but many others too. "When doctors know a patient is going to make it, that's when I can go in and talk with them, and talk with the family. I've talked with mothers of babies who've had their child burned from something as simple as wiping up their high chair with a hot rag just to sanitize it and set the baby down on it—just because that plastic held that heat. The mother is devastated. Do I know anything about how to take care of a baby who's been burned? No. But I was there for the mother—just someone to talk to, and to let her know that things happen. The doctor is saying the baby is going to be fine, but at the time, that's not helping her—she just needs someone to talk to who has been there.

"It is one thing for a doctor to tell someone they will recover, but it's something entirely different for someone like me, who has been through what they are going through, to provide support and assure them that they will indeed recover," Dave said. "This important component of recovery was something that I never had when I was burned, so I vowed to never let anyone go through that experience alone if I can help it."

About a third of the kids at burn camp come from low-income backgrounds, and that experience got Dave thinking about what else he could do to help with other needs in their lives. "We started asking ourselves what else we could do for these young burn patients. We were helping them at burn camp and at Loyola's medical center, but we were losing track of them when they turned 17 or 18."

One thing he saw was that many of the kids wouldn't have the opportunity to go to college. "You could just see the wheels were spinning in his head on what he could do to make a difference," says Werderitch.

That thought led Dave and Michele to start a nonprofit organization of their own, the From Tragedy to Triumph Foundation, which raises funds to award college scholarships to burn survivors. The foundation dispensed $120,000 in scholarship awards in its first five years of operation, ranging from $1,500 to $5,500. They run the foundation together, and they are part of a broad local and national burn community that provides a great deal of mutual support and sustenance.

Dave and Michele's process of recovery and transformation has been very much a slow, step-by-step process. In fact, they didn't start the foundation until 10 years after Dave's accident. Dave and Michele had traveled to Washington, D.C., where they were honored with a Jefferson Award for their outstanding volunteer work with SOAR and at burn camp. "We met so many other people who were doing tremendous things with their lives, and it inspired us to start thinking about what else we could do," Dave explains. That's when the idea for scholarships to help young burn victims surfaced.

Dave and Michele's relationship also went through change—and not only because of the explosion. Dave's accident actually was the first of two traumas that would rock their world. Two years after Dave's injury, Michele was standing in her kitchen one Saturday morning baking cookies with their younger daughter, Brittany, when a hospital in Billings, Montana, called with the news that their daughter Chrisele, a freshman at the University of Montana, had sustained life-threatening brain injuries in a serious automobile accident. Difficult as the burns had been, Chrisele's accident was much more traumatic.

Returning from an outing with a friend, Chrisele had lost control of the car; the investigation didn't turn up a definite cause, and Chrisele couldn't remember what happened. But the vehicle rolled over seven times. Her friend had broken bones and cuts, but Chrisele had suffered an injury that caused acute damage to her frontal lobe, the part of the brain that handles executive functioning, planning, and organizing. She was in a coma for two and a half weeks. "We didn't know if Chrisele was ever going to wake up," Dave says.

Chrisele's only other serious physical injuries were a dislocated left elbow and a lost left ear, which would be replaced later with a prosthetic. But her cognitive recovery was a difficult five-year process. She had difficulty with speech and expressive language, and had a good deal of memory loss.

"She would sit on the couch for hours doing puzzle books, just to keep that brain going," Dave recalls. Later, Chrisele was able to resume her education, taking whatever classes she could at a local community college. Ironically, she had always been interested in going into medicine, and had an interest in neurology. She ultimately was able to graduate from nursing school in 2011, nine years after her accident. She is a nurse in a brain injury unit at the prestigious Rehabilitation Institute of Chicago, is married, and has young twin boys.

The multiple traumas endured by the Schury family add an unusual twist to the one-foot-in-front-of-the-other nature of post-traumatic growth. The family learned about resilience, recovery, and growth from the horrific burns Dave suffered and were able to use their newfound resourcefulness when trauma struck a second time.

"My burn injury just prepared us for what was about to really happen," Dave says. "Michele had to go through my accident alone and with the kids. But when Chrisele got hurt, we had both of us to pick each other up when one of us was down. You just hope that you both won't be down at the same time. We thought my accident was so devastating, and then Chrisele gets hurt—and mine is nothing compared with what she had to go through to recover."

"This was a big concern that was always on my mind—whether our marriage and family life could sustain these tragedies," Michele says. "We always had such a great relationship, and we'd just keep working at it. Don't get me wrong, there were times when I wanted to pack my bags and leave because I couldn't take it anymore. It was hard for both of us."

The strength of their relationship has played a big part, along with the great support they have received from their families and neighbors, and their story underscores the importance of mutually supportive relationships when one partner has—or both have—experienced a traumatic jolt.

Dave and Michele are careful to say that their healing and growth happened gradually. Dave would never have found his way to working with burn victims if his accident hadn't happened. His interest in it developed organically—in a series of steps he took during recovery. "It's not like we woke up one day and said, 'Okay, tragedy is behind us,'" says Michele. "You live with it your entire life—you just live differently. There isn't a moment where someone comes knocking on your door and says, 'This is where we're going to lead you.'"

How do spouses affect the process of change? The interplay of married couples is just starting to emerge as a topic in psychological research about post-traumatic growth. University of North Carolina psychologist Amy Canevello and two colleagues wanted to study the role of responsiveness in the post-traumatic growth experienced by romantic partners, so they studied the relationships of 61 married couples from a small Midwestern city who had experienced severe damage to their homes due to flooding. They found that close relationships may play a key role in fostering post-traumatic growth, and that the process of mutual and personal growth can be passed from one to another. "Relationships become stronger and better, and it makes sense that when that happens, you would be more attuned to a partner's needs," Canevello says. "You are more caring, validating them and understanding them...and if I perceive that my partner cares and is validating me, that promotes my growth."

Canevello thinks this process of post-traumatic growth "contagion" also occurs in cases where only one partner has experienced the trauma. And the process isn't limited to romantic couples, she says. "I don't have any reason to think you wouldn't see this process happening in other close relationships—parents and children or very close friends or siblings. It's less about a romantic partner than it is about people you are close with, who you have intimacy with and can count on."

Like Dave and Michele Schury, Mark and Cheryl Kaplan survived a jolt that forced them to change as a couple together. On the night of June 11, 2011, Mark and Cheryl had just returned to their suburban Chicago home from a night at the movies when Mark answered the phone. "I knew instantly from the tone of Mark's voice that whatever was being discussed was not good," Cheryl remembers. "I thought, 'Just hang up and make it go away.'" The news was heart-stopping: their daughter Hannah, a college junior studying in a semester-abroad program in Chile, had fallen from a second-story window of a hostel in the town of Valparaiso in a freak accident caused by a faulty railing. She had sustained severe, life-threatening head injuries. Although it was too late at night to call family and friends, Hannah's younger siblings, Sophie and Charlie, came home to hear the shocking news. Mark, a physician, kicked into overdrive, making travel arrangements, researching the hospital where Hannah had been taken, and refreshing his medical knowledge of brain injury. "The rest of us just curled up into the fetal position for hours waiting for news," Cheryl recalls.

Mark and Cheryl took the first possible flight from Chicago; by the time they arrived in Valparaiso, Hannah had undergone two surgeries and was in an induced coma while doctors worked to relieve pressure in her brain. She was also fighting a lung infection. She was comatose, almost unrecognizable, on a respirator, and fighting for her life. She was hospitalized for a month in Chile, with Cheryl and Mark at her bedside. They had plenty of support from staff at Hannah's university, Washington University in St. Louis, and from the local Jewish community; people read about the accident in the press and started showing up at the hospital to offer help. Hannah was flown home on a specially equipped private plane, accompanied by medical staff, and went straight to a hospital intensive care unit, then to the Rehabilitation Institute of Chicago for another month as an inpatient. "They put her in a program for the least hopeful cases, because the outlook was so grim," Cheryl says. "But they took her, and she started outperforming everyone's wildest expectations in terms of her improvement."

Hannah was fortunate to survive the traumatic brain injury at all, but more than that, she made an excellent recovery. A year after the injury, she was able to eat, talk, read, and write. One of Hannah's first steps back into independent life was signing up for a Spanish class at a local community college, mainly to see how she would acclimate to getting back into the routine of being in a classroom and sitting through a lecture and learning to commute by bus. "I drove her at first, then we took a bus together, then she took the bus alone," Cheryl remembers. "Can you imagine not being sure if your 21-year-old daughter could take a bus ride by herself? But it was huge."

Hannah returned to Washington University, graduating with a degree in Spanish two years later. Although she struggles with memory issues, she has been able to work as a teaching assistant in a preschool and lives independently.

Fighting to save their daughter's life, Mark and Cheryl found a balance. "There was a little bit of divide and conquer because of Mark's profession," Cheryl says. "He could navigate the medical aspect of what we were dealing with, which was extremely helpful when medical jargon needed to be translated or we were researching healthcare facilities or doctors. I would take care of more of the day-to-day help that Hannah needed—social services, activities of daily living, things we needed in the house, when she could go back to school."

The Kaplans now consider themselves very lucky, and together they experienced positive changes in the aftermath of Hannah's injury and near-death. Cheryl, a professional grant writer for nonprofit organizations, wound up leaving that work behind and has been learning to do floral design. She finds the work calming. "It brings me to a peaceful place that I wasn't getting in work at a desk," she says. Mark, an allergist with a private practice, finds that he doesn't get stressed out as easily as he did before the injury. "When you go through something like this where you almost lose a child, your idea about what constitutes a tragedy changes," he says. "My overall perspective on things has changed. A lot of stuff rolls off my back that didn't before. I have a new perspective on what is important...I feel mindful of what is important and what isn't." He also feels more cognizant of the passage of time and is more focused on spending time with family. "My life has always been family-centered, but maybe I'm more that way now than before. I just take fewer things for granted than I used to."

Of course, trauma can set the stage for distress in a relationship, too. Cheryl acknowledges the risk: "I can easily see how this kind of experience could go the other way for a couple," she says. "There were just so many things we had to try to agree on. I think we acknowledged that this could bring us together or it could tear us apart—which do we want it to be? We each wanted to do this together as a team. But I think this helped our communication skills as a couple, and getting through it together was reinforcing for our relationship."

The emotional support they were able to provide to one another was a part of the "yin and yang" that Mark describes as their process of recovery. "Early on, we took turns losing our shit. We would hold each other up. It's pretty profound to go through this with a life partner—it's extremely helpful emotionally that you have someone you can depend on and who can depend on you."

Amanda North came of age in suburban New York City in the 1970s. She grew up in a family of travelers; her grandparents' Wisconsin farmhouse was filled with artifacts from all over the world, and her mother also was an avid collector of objects. But Amanda also had an early interest in politics and the world. "I just ran across my high school yearbook from ninth grade—how many kids do you know who would answer the question, 'What do you want to be when you grow up?' with this: 'Ambassadress to Red China,'" she tells me with a laugh.

Talk with her today, and imagining that high school kid isn't difficult. Amanda is smart, articulate, and warm. But when she began her career in the 1980s, she didn't head to China. Rather, she went to work in Silicon Valley, doing stints at Apple and later for wireless communications and software companies in the Bay Area. The work was good, and paid well—important for a divorced mother raising two kids. But it often felt like a long detour from her aspirations coming out of school to make a difference in the world. "Somehow life takes its course, and you can go off on paths that take you further and further away from what you really believe in and want—often for good reasons," she says.

By 2012, Amanda found herself working as head of marketing for a producer of telecom wireless infrastructure products. Her frustrations with the tech world were growing, and she was feeling burned out.

She began exploring possible new career paths by doing volunteer work as a mentor in a program for would-be entrepreneurs at Santa Clara University in San Jose. The mentor program connects Silicon Valley executives with entrepreneurs in regions with developing economies, and had done work with several groups in India working on sustainability for small villages, partly through focusing on developing markets for artisan crafts. That connected with Amanda's own interest in artisan goods. She had started traveling with her teenaged children, visiting destinations like Cambodia, Peru, Brazil, Belize, Turkey, Morocco, Kenya, and Vietnam. "I was already divorced, and I thought traveling with them would be a way to spend quality time together, and to get away from digital media, Facebook, and cellphones," she says. A favorite travel activity was visiting local artisans, and many of them were worried about their futures. "You could see that ways of life were changing in the villages we'd visit, and as someone interested in culture and anthropology, that saddened me," she says. In the Indian city of Udaipur, Amanda and her daughter Lili got into a conversation with a textile merchant whose family had been in business since the sixteenth century. "He told me his kids were in America and didn't care about the business, and that the business was going to die when he did."

All of this rumination meant that Amanda's life was primed for change on April 15, 2013.

A little before 3:00 p.m. that day, Amanda was standing near the finish line of the Boston Marathon, waiting for her daughter to cross.

Lili, a sophomore at Harvard, was coming in about an hour after the first runners crossed. Bruce Springsteen's "Born to Run" was blaring over the loudspeakers, and the crowd was in a great mood. "I remember thinking that this was one of the happiest moments in my life," Amanda says. "I knew Lili would be crossing in a couple minutes, and I was tearing up with the emotion of being there."

The next moment, Amanda was thrown to the ground by the force of an explosion. Instantly, she was enveloped by thick smoke and noticed embers burning on her coat and trousers. "I started looking around and saw a man with two severed legs—he was conscious but had no legs at all. I very rationally said to myself, 'I can't do anything for him.' I looked to my left and saw a young woman with a huge gaping hole in her left calf, and I thought maybe I could help her. It was a series of detached thoughts, like watching someone else in a movie. Then the second bomb went off, and I thought, 'It's like 9/11, and we are under attack.'"

She crept a couple of feet over to the woman, took her own coat off and put it over her, hoping to keep her out of shock. She recalled that her grandfather, who was a surgeon, had told her it was important to keep an injured person calm and try to keep him or her out of shock. She started yelling loudly to get help, and a young man who turned out to be a veteran responded. They used Amanda's belt as a tourniquet to stop the young woman's bleeding. It took a while for Amanda to realize that she had been injured too. She had a deep cut on one leg, and the other had third-degree burns. Her eardrums were perforated, and bits from one of the bombs were fused to her hair.

Amanda started to panic about her daughter as she was being wheeled into a medical tent on a gurney. No one was sure how big the blast had been, and cellphone service was down. Only later would it become clear that the bombs planted by Chechen brothers Dzhokhar and Tamerlan Tsarnaev had killed three people and injured 260 others.

Lili had been spared serious injury. Running with a friend, they had both been thrown off their feet but picked themselves up and took shelter in a building. Amanda and Lili reconnected in the hospital. "It was an emotional moment—Lili said we had been spared by a miracle and our lives would never be the same."

The bombing served as a sort of mental turbocharge that brought Amanda's thinking about her work front and center. The brush with death "snapped things back into position," she says. "Lili and I were sitting in the hospital that night, talking about how you never know how much time you will have left on this earth, and I just had an overwhelming sense of gratitude that we were both alive, and a desire to start living with passion and purpose. When I thought about the big problems I had seen, I kept coming back to the artisans, and asking myself what I could bring to that—maybe there was something I could do." From there, she quickly decided to leave her job to launch Artisan Connect. "Literally, the neural pathways connected and the idea came together within 48 hours," Amanda says.

Artisan Connect is an e-commerce website that aims to provide access to wider, Western markets for artisans in developing countries. Amanda's goal is to help artisans in remote locations thrive by giving them not only revenue but, fair prices and profits. The company works with artisan groups in Latin America, India, Indonesia, and South Africa. Amanda's staff of four work on distributing high-end home furnishings, selling mainly to interior designers and consumers. The company specializes in handcrafted tabletop items, home decorations, blankets, and pillows. "We start with beautiful products and back that up with a social cause," she says. "Our focus is on people who don't want to buy a lot of stuff, but want to buy things with intent."

A trip had taken Amanda to Bhuj, a small city on the western edge of India, about 18 miles from the border with Pakistan. Handicrafts have always been a key part of the local economy, but even more so in the aftermath of a major earthquake in 2001 that killed 20,000 people and destroyed about 400,000 homes. "In India, artisans traditionally have been one of the lower castes, and hence more vulnerable to economic disruption," Amanda would later write about the trip in a post for a blog she maintained at the time. "So, in the aftermath of the earthquake, the Indian government funded the Khamir Craft Center to strengthen and promote local handicrafts and preserve the relationship with the environment. The district is renowned for its crafts, particularly textiles and intricate embroidery. Each village boasts its own design tradition. Tiny mirrors are stitched into many of the pieces—lore has it to scare off the lions and leopards that still inhabit this arid countryside. We were fascinated by the intricate process whereby wool from local herds and locally grown organic cotton are colored with organic dyes made from berries and nuts. Deeper blue is achieved using cow urine—who knew?"

Although Amanda's process of change was far shorter than that of the Schurys or the Kaplans, the urge to take her life in a totally new direction didn't just surface, fully formed that evening in the Boston hospital. Instead, strands of her previous life became fused together in a new way. The attack pushed her to adopt a fuller view of herself. "I had just gotten far away from the things that mattered to me," she says. Although Amanda remembers this as a "lightbulb" moment, the change really had been brewing for a long time. And while the near-miss trauma in Boston shook her to the core, she was thinking clearly that night in the hospital.

Amanda recovered fully from her physical wounds from the bombing. These days, she still travels several times a year to meet artisans. "It's soul-satisfying and reminds me why I am doing this in the first place," she says.

For Frank Smyth, the process of post-traumatic growth and transformation stretched over a seven-year period. Frank is a tough guy with a long, distinguished career as an independent investigative journalist specializing in armed conflicts, organized crime, and human rights, reporting on topics like genocide in Guatemala and Columbian paramilitary operations. He has contributed work to CBS News, *The Nation*, *The Village Voice*, *The New Republic*, *The Washington Post*, *The New York Times*, and many other news outlets.

In March of 1991, Frank was in Iraq covering the Kurdish uprising following the Gulf War. He and his colleagues were ambushed by the Iraqi army outside the town of Kirkuk, and one of Frank's colleagues, Gad Gross, a Romanian-born photographer working for *Newsweek* magazine, was shot and killed. Frank and French photographer Alain Buu were captured at gunpoint and held in the Abu Ghraib prison, where they witnessed torture, were interrogated, and were accused of spying. "The most difficult feeling was our abject helplessness as we listened to the cries of other prisoners being abused," Smyth later wrote.

"The guards' instrument of choice was a heavy rubber hose. We listened and occasionally managed to watch—I could just peek out a small window that looked into the prison yard—as men were beaten. Prisoners were made to hold out their hands just like in Catholic grade school. Some were hit in the soles of the feet. If a prisoner raised his hand to defend himself, he would be savagely beaten about the head and body.

"The guards also had a collection of heavy sticks, some as thick and twice as long as a baseball bat. I watched one blindfolded man beaten with these sticks in the cellblock yard. About five guards surrounded him, flailing away, as the prisoner tried to remove his blindfold. One ingeniously sadistic guard playfully held a broom handle like a pool cue and repeatedly poked a crying man in the head."

Frank and his colleague were released after 18 days in prison, and he soon went back to work, pushing emotions about his experiences into a corner of his mind. He was carrying a tremendous sense of guilt about what had happened, because he had insisted on staying where they were despite the dangers, and a feeling that he had abdicated his responsibility for leading the group of journalists and keeping them safe. This went on for seven years—and bottling up the trauma took Frank down some dark paths: smoking, drinking and doing drugs, and philandering. "I was not a happy, well-adjusted human being," he remembers. "I was drinking, smoking dope, and womanizing—just experiencing a great degree of self-alienation." He was doing well professionally but was in denial about what had happened to him in Iraq. "I could focus and channel my energy into my work, but I was broken," he says.

Frank started to come to terms with himself only when he entered therapy and started getting acupuncture treatments. Around the same time, he got involved in the Dart Center for Journalism & Trauma at the Columbia Journalism School, which works with journalists covering trauma. One of Dart's roles is to educate journalists about trauma, how to cover it and how to deal with the psychological effects of exposure to it. Becoming a fellow at Dart in 1999, Frank started to realize the extent of his full-blown traumatic stress syndrome, and that he had been walking around with it for eight years.

"It was only when I became a Dart fellow that I started to realize that I had full-blown PTSD and had had it for eight years. I started to realize I wanted to take control of my own process of treatment." Frank started doing yoga and became interested in Buddhism and meditation. All of those steps—especially therapy—helped him to stop bottling up the guilt he felt about Gad's death and the trauma he was walking around with due to the torture he had witnessed.

Frank later found a path to purpose when he founded Global Journalist Security (GJS), a consulting firm that trains journalists and workers at nongovernmental organizations on how to operate in hostile environments around the world. GJS is made up of veteran journalists like Smyth, but also press freedom advocates and security-training professionals. It focuses on training to help journalists and nongovernmental organization workers navigate in theaters of war and deal with targeting by criminals and the risk of sexual assault. There's also an "emotional self-care" component, including training modules on resilience, stress release, and coping with trauma.

The direct line from Frank's experience in Iraq to his work today is obvious, but the meaning and healing are less visible on the surface. "I used to get choked up when I talked about my own experiences, but now I rarely do," he says. "The process of what I've given back over the past 15 years has helped me process that."

The work Frank does today has given his life a new sense of meaning, he adds. It's the key to understanding the slow-burning process of transformation he underwent. "As a journalist, I was much better at nailing the bad guys than doing anything for the good guys. I had the excitement of getting a big story published, I could have parties, I was cool. But I had to get past that."

Frank experienced a prolonged period of guilt and shame over what occurred in Iraq, but he accepts it now. "What you want is not guilt and shame, but remorse and healing—and transformation," he says. "I'm not grateful for what occurred, and I'm not regretful—but I accept it, and I accept my responsibility, and I heal myself from it. I can help people, I've realized—people who need training and support, and who might be going through what I experienced. Ultimately, I'm a more whole, complete, and likable human being."

CHAPTER FIVE

THE ROLE OF FAITH AND SPIRITUALITY

Many jolt survivors experience a heightened sense of spiritual awakening and growth—connected to a specific belief in a higher being or to a deeper sense of being alive and connected to family, friends, community, and the world. What roles do faith and spirituality play in transformations following trauma?

Robert Grant, a clinical psychologist who has specialized in trauma, cross-cultural issues, and spirituality for over 30 years, writes in an essay that trauma survivors are by definition "overwhelmed and rendered helpless." He continues: "Trauma initiates a process of deep spiritual questioning and demands that victims take in more of reality than was previously possible...Trauma, in spite of its brutality and destructiveness, has the power to open victims to issues of profound existential and spiritual significance...Trauma throws victims onto a path that mystics, shamans, mythic heroes and spiritual seekers have been walking for thousands of years. The difference is that victims of trauma must work this territory or be overcome by it."

Eva Leivas-Andino describes such a spiritual awakening following the emotional trauma of her son Paolo's coming out as gay, and what she views as her initial failure to provide him with the support he needed.

"It was the first step in my realizing who I am," she says. "It just opened the floodgates. I now have a theory that if you're awake, your spirituality is always being transformed...I know I have been awake, so I have been transformed and changed. Every night when I go to bed, I hear on the news that the world is coming to an end and there is nothing we can do. But every morning, I wake up and think, 'Today I'm going to make a difference.' That is the most empowering feeling you can ever have in your life. It freed me, because when you drop the fear, when you are truly free of fear, there is no holding you back. There is nothing I can't do. I have a purpose that fills my life."

Are religious people most likely to experience post-traumatic growth? The experts are, let's say, agnostic on the subject. "It's hard to answer," says psychologist Lawrence Calhoun. "If a person tells me their faith drove their growth, I'd want a lot more information. But if your view of religion is generally positive, it certainly can help you cope generally with trauma. Is it connected with post-traumatic growth? Perhaps." Calhoun adds that some trauma survivors become angry with God, asking why God would allow something terrible to happen. But strong faith often is impervious to trauma, Calhoun and his colleague Richard Tedeschi have found. "Religious beliefs are robust, and it can be very difficult or impossible for life events to disconfirm them," says Calhoun. "A person's belief in God, although perhaps shaken by what happens, is not directly contradicted by any set of life circumstances."

Religious belief can provide a way for survivors of trauma to assimilate and process a traumatic event, and guide people to a positive growth experience. Consider Bill Pelke, who co-founded the anti-death penalty organization Journey of Hope with Marietta Jaeger, whose young daughter was murdered. An Indiana steelworker, Bill became a leading international figure in the fight to end the death penalty after the brutal murder of his grandmother on May 14, 1985, by four teenage girls in Gary, Indiana. The girls—one was 16, two were 15, and one was just 14 years old—had planned to rob Ruth Pelke, a 77-year-old Bible-school teacher, for a few dollars to play video games. They gained entry to the trusting Mrs. Pelke's home by telling her they wanted to sign up for her Bible-school class. The plan went bad and they panicked, striking their victim in the head with a flower vase and stabbing her 33 times with a kitchen knife before running off with $10 and the keys to Ruth's car. One of the four girls convicted of the crime, Paula Cooper, was sentenced to death at age 16, becoming the youngest person in the United States ever sent to death row. (Under Indiana law at the time, juveniles as young as age 10 could be charged as adults.)

At the time, Bill was a crane operator at Bethlehem Steel in northwest Indiana. He's a big, barrel-chested man with an intense gaze that you could mistake for anger, and he comes off a bit gruff until you get to know him a bit. He doesn't look like someone you'd pick from Central Casting for a role as an anti-death penalty activist.

Bill was raised as a very conservative Baptist. "When I graduated college, Jerry Falwell delivered our commencement speech, and we thought he was pretty liberal," he says with a laugh. Bill was a radio operator in Vietnam, where he served for a year. He saw plenty of mayhem and gore there—fellow soldiers killed, and friends with legs and other body parts shot off. He came home with three pieces of shrapnel lodged in the right side of his back, under his armpit.

Paula Cooper was sent to death row just over a year after the murder, in July of 1986. Bill was at peace with the sentence. After all, he had gone through the ordeal of seeing his father and a cousin scrub his grandmother's blood from the walls and carpet of her house. "I knew we had a death penalty in this country, and different people were being sentenced to death for various crimes. I felt that if other people were being given the death penalty for murder, then they should give the death penalty to the girl who murdered my grandmother," he recalls. But, fighting back tears that day, he also said this about the death sentence to a reporter at the courthouse: "It won't bring back my grandmother."

After Paula's sentencing, Bill found himself reflecting on his grandmother's life and death. He didn't consider himself a very religious person, but he found himself turning back to his faith for guidance. "I began to ask my God why, why did he allow one of his most precious angels to suffer such a horrendous death? Why did our family—a good family—have to suffer that way?" He also found himself thinking about his grandmother's strong Christian belief, and also about Jesus's Sermon on the Mount, especially Matthew 18:21-22: "Then Peter came to Jesus and asked, 'Lord, how many times shall I forgive my brother when he sins against me? Up to seven times?' Jesus answered, 'I tell you, not seven times, but 70 times seven.'

"When I thought about that, I knew he was saying forgiveness should be a habit," Bill says, "a way of life—to forgive, to forgive, and to forgive, and keep on forgiving."

Everything came to a head for Bill around November—just a few months after Paula's sentencing. He found himself thinking constantly about the case, and was praying for understanding of the brutal crime and how he should respond. Working a shift one evening, he was sitting 50 feet in the air in the cab of his crane at the steel mill, waiting for other workers to arrive. He would write later: "The only time I had done much praying during the previous 10 years was when Nana had been killed, but these last few weeks I was almost praying without ceasing. I had been involved in what I called anguishing prayer." Tears were streaming down his face. "I thought to myself, 'Paula Cooper didn't know what she was doing—someone that knows what they're doing doesn't take a 12-inch butcher knife and stab someone 33 times. What happened that day was a crazy, senseless act.' And I thought, 'I think my faith is telling me to forgive.' And I said to myself, 'Maybe someday I will.' But as I thought about my grandmother, I envisioned a picture that had been taken before her death, that had been in all the newspapers, a very beautiful picture. And as I sat in the crane, I began to envision that picture, but with tears in her eyes—and I knew they were tears of love and compassion. I thought about the trial, and how when the judge began to read the verdict of death, Paula's grandfather began to wail and cry, 'They're going to kill my baby; they're going to kill my baby,' and I watched him as he left the room with tears streaming down his cheeks. And I knew my grandmother would not want this grandfather to have to see a granddaughter who he loved very much strapped to an electric chair and volts of electricity go through her body until she was dead."

Bill prayed to God for the love and compassion he needed to forgive Paula. As he sat in the crane, he started to think that he could write her a letter sharing his grandmother's faith and how she had lived, and he began to feel that God had touched his heart. He says he came down from that crane a changed man, and he believes fervently to this day that what he experienced that evening was a miracle. "I knew when I came down the crane stairs that day and left the job, my life was going to be different, although I really didn't know how. From that moment on, I wouldn't picture how my grandmother died, but how she lived, and what she stood for." He made two promises to God that night: first, that he would walk through any door of opportunity that opened to him to share what he had learned. Second, that he would never take any credit for his successes, but would "give God the honor and the glory," because any achievements would not be his own.

Shortly after his night of prayer on the crane, Bill ran into an old friend. Talking about the Cooper case, the friend said, "I hope that bitch burns."

"It was a way that other people used to express sympathy to me," Bill says. "But I just shrugged my shoulders, looked at him, and said: 'I don't.'" Bill's friend looked surprised, even offended, but told him that he ought to let other people know how he felt. So Bill submitted a short op-ed article to Northwest Indiana's *Post-Tribune*, titled "The Answer Is":

The answer is love, prayer and forgiveness. Ruth E. Pelke lived and died knowing the right answer. She knew the Way and followed it.

Why would God allow such a horrendous death to one of His most precious children? There can only be one answer and that answer is revival. We need revival in this country...

Preachers—God is long-suffering and He is ready to pour His Spirit. He is ready for a revival. Now is the time for revival in the hearts of man. How do we reach hearts? Through the children. Children are our future. Children are most important.

God allowed Mrs. Pelke's murder. Why? Could it be that God knew the case of Paula Cooper would gain the eye of the world? Could it be that He knew the ears of the world would be eager to hear what Paula might say? Paula Cooper can start revival fire by singing of the Glory of God.

Pray for Paula Cooper.

Love Paula Cooper.

Forgive Paula Cooper.

Paula Cooper is seeking a closer relationship with God and she has God's love and forgiveness. How about yours? She has mine. Ruth Pelke would want it that Way. I am her grandson.

Bill didn't know what kind of reaction his essay might prompt, but soon after it was published, he ran into a cousin who told him she had read it and that she didn't want to see Paula executed either. Bill told her about his experience in the crane. "She seemed a bit skeptical when I first began to describe that experience," he wrote later in his book, *Journey of Hope...From Violence to Healing*, "but by the time I was finished, we were both in tears and hugging each other." Bill kept checking the newspaper for letters to the editor after his essay ran, but strangely enough, the piece seemed to put a halt to the community discussion of the issue. "All letters about Nana, Paula, and the death penalty stopped. There was no dialogue at all," he wrote.

Elsewhere, the discussion was just getting started. Ruth's murder and Paula's death row sentence continued to gain notoriety; in many parts of the world, the response was outrage at the idea of executing someone as young as Paula. A series about the case in an Italian newspaper generated especially strong interest, and Amnesty International campaigned to get her off death row. Ultimately, a petition signed by 2 million people seeking a commuted sentence reached the Indiana Supreme Court. Pope John Paul II sent a Vatican emissary to Indiana to plead for her life. Bill, who had become deeply involved in the campaign to save Paula's life, fasted, prayed, and did television interviews—he even traveled to Italy on her behalf.

Bill's battles on behalf of Paula, and against the death penalty, have come at considerable cost. Bill already was divorced from his first wife, Mary, in 1984—a year before the murder—and his three teenaged children lived nearby. A woman he was dating at the time, Judy, thought

Bill was "crazy" when he first forgave Paula; she could not understand his opposition to the death penalty, Bill says. She later came around to Bill's point of view and the two married, but the union lasted less than a decade. "She decided she didn't want to be the wife of an activist husband who would be traveling around the country, and suddenly to my shock and dismay abruptly left the marriage," Bill says. Many of Bill's friends and members of the Gary community didn't understand what he was doing, and there were rifts in the family. Just before he left for Rome in May 1987, the local newspaper ran an article quoting Bill's father: "I believe my son is one of the so-called new breed who doesn't feel you should have to pay your debts. That is contrary to my philosophy." Bill told the reporter: "My grandmother died a martyr for Jesus Christ, and Christ forgave his enemies. My grandmother would want us to do the same."

Bill has spent his life since Paula's conviction traveling the world telling the story of his personal journey of forgiving Paula and trying to get her off death row. He retired from Bethlehem Steel in 1997 and has devoted much of his life to campaigning against the death penalty. He is an organizer of the Abolitionist Action Committee, which for 23 years has held a four-day fast and vigil outside the U.S. Supreme Court to protest the death penalty. The event begins each year on June 29, the anniversary of the 1972 *Furman v. Georgia* decision, which halted executions in the United States; the event ends on July 2, the anniversary of the 1976 *Gregg v. Georgia* decision, which allowed executions to resume. Every year, he organizes a two-week Journey of Hope tour that pulls together an extraordinary group of family members of murder victims and of the accused, as well as people who have been exonerated from death row sentences.

Bill developed an extraordinary relationship with Paula Cooper that began with an exchange of letters in 1986. "I wrote to her saying that I wanted to visit her and share a few things I thought my grandmother would want me to share with her from the Bible. I didn't know if she'd write back, but about 10 days later I got a letter from her, but the prison rules prohibited a visit between a perpetrator of a violent crime and the victim's family." Instead, they exchanged letters every 10 days or so for the next eight years, when a visit finally was approved. Here's how Bill describes that first visit, which took place on Thanksgiving Day of 1994, in his book:

"I remembered what Paula said [in a television documentary] about wanting to look me in the eye and know for sure that I had forgiven her. I was in the visitor's room when Paula came in. I stood up and she came over to me. At the other prisons I had visited, you were allowed to give a hug at the start and end of a visit. I asked Paula if it was okay if I gave her a hug. She said, "Yes." I gave a short hug, took a step back, looked her in the eyes and said, "I love you and have forgiven you."

Paula and I had exchanged dozens of letters over the years. Many of mine talked about forgiveness. Paula had read a lot of articles about me talking about forgiveness. But if she wanted to look me in the eyes to know for sure, it was fine with me.

We talked about a lot of things. We talked about people we knew in common [in the criminal justice system and advocacy community]. We talked about the traveling that I had been doing...We talked about the people on death row and she told me how glad she was that I had shifted my efforts from helping her to helping them.

We did not talk about Nana or her death. We did talk a little about God, the Bible, and prayer. Before I knew it, our one-hour visit was over. It was time to go. I gave her a good-bye hug and told her once again that I loved her.

As I drove home, I felt more like I was floating or flying than driving. One word kept going over and over in my mind, the word *wonderful.* Whenever I began to sum up the day in my mind, the word *wonderful* jumped out at me.

Why *wonderful?* I had just visited with someone who had done a terrible thing to somebody I deeply loved, someone who had hurt my entire family immensely, someone who I would have had all the reasons in the world to hate and have the desire for revenge. Yet I had none of those feelings.

I had feelings of love, compassion, and forgiveness. It *was* wonderful. I praised God for those feelings as I drove home. It was truly a *wonderful* Thanksgiving Day.

I felt that was how God wanted us to love each of His children that way, and to me it was wonderful."

Paula was taken off death row in 1989 following a long court battle and an international outcry against the state's plan to execute an adolescent; her sentence was commuted to 60 years in prison. While in prison, she completed a General Equivalency Degree and ultimately a college degree. She took gourmet-cooking classes and cooked often for the prison staff.

132

She was released from prison on parole in June 2013. Paula had served just over 26 years in prison. Bill and Paula had grown close over the years, but he was told by the prison board that Paula was not permitted to have in-person contact with the victim's family. They communicated frequently via a special email system for prisoners during Paula's re-entry to society, and Bill tried to be as helpful as he could as she looked for work and tried to adjust to life outside prison. But two years after her release, Paula was dead.

"I got the news the day after Memorial Day that she had committed suicide," Bill remembers with tears streaming down his face. "It was a terrible day for me—a terrible day for a lot of people. Paula was going to join the Journey of Hope and show how people could change, but she found it so hard when she got out of prison that people were not forgiving of what she had done. She felt she had done her time, but everyone still wanted to hold this against her. I still can't talk about it, but I know I did the right thing. The answer is love and compassion for all humanity. And if you have love and compassion for all of humanity, you're not going to see anyone put in the death chamber and their life taken from them. It's impossible."

The command to forgive seemed crystal clear to Bill, but religious faith sometimes complicates things for jolt survivors. Lucy McBath is an evangelical Christian who finds herself politically at odds with much of her own religious movement over one of the most divisive political issues in the United States: gun control. Lucy became a nationally known advocate for gun control following the horrifying murder of her teenaged son, Jordan Davis, in one of the best-known white-on-black shootings in recent years. Jordan's killer, Michael David Dunn, attempted to defend himself in court using the infamous Florida self-defense statute known as Stand Your Ground. Enacted in 2005, the statute authorizes people to protect and defend themselves against threats or perceived threats, using any level of force they judge necessary, without any duty to retreat.

Dunn was a gun owner and member of the National Rifle Association with an alleged history of angry outbursts. He kept a 9mm semiautomatic weapon in his glove compartment with two loaded magazines. He would later claim that he was prompted to pull out the gun because he felt threatened by the boys and that he thought he saw a shotgun through the window of the SUV that Jordan and his friends were in (though no shotgun was found). Dunn fired 10 shots into the SUV, killing Jordan; his three friends managed to escape unharmed. Dunn and his girlfriend went back to their hotel, where he ordered a pizza and went to sleep. He was arrested the next morning, two hours away from the scene of the shooting.

The state of Florida has been a sort of test laboratory for the NRA's efforts nationally to weaken gun control, having passed numerous laws over the past two decades that chip away at restrictions. Independent research studies have found that Stand Your Ground laws don't deter crime but do lead to a statistically significant increase in the number of reported murders and non-negligent manslaughters. Urban Institute researchers found that the laws have a disparate racial impact: when white shooters kill African-American victims, 34 percent of the homicides are deemed justifiable, compared to just 3.3 percent when blacks kill whites.

Like Bill Pelke, Lucy says she ultimately felt compelled to forgive Dunn—"one of the most difficult things in my life, ever," she says. But more important was her feeling that she was being called to make a change in her own life. "I understood there was something more that I was supposed to do that was important, that God was speaking to me."

Since Jordan's murder, Lucy has transformed herself into a national leader in the fight for gun control. She established a scholarship fund in Jordan's name, and she is working with former President Barack Obama's My Brother's Keeper initiative. Lucy is one of the "Mothers of the Movement"—a small group of mothers of black men and women who have either been killed by gun violence or in violent encounters with police officers. Along with Lucy, they include the mothers of Trayvon Martin, Sandra Bland, Eric Garner, and Dontre Hamilton. Lucy today is a full-time staff member of Everytown for Gun Safety, one of the key national organizations fighting for gun control. Although she comes from a political family, she wasn't much engaged in politics before Jordan's murder. She worked most of her career as a flight attendant for Delta Airlines, and that's how she was earning a living at the time of the shooting. "I was always very politically aware of what was going on in the country, but not really putting that awareness into action," she tells me.

That changed immediately after the murder. "I wanted to tell Jordan's story—we didn't want anyone speaking for us. No one could really speak to what was happening in the country, because we were the victims. I started speaking out very early after Jordan's death about the implicit bias, racism, and gun violence and how it tied together into that cauldron that caused Jordan's death."

Lucy's activism began with a gun violence prevention rally near the Martin Luther King, Jr. Center for Nonviolent Social Change in Atlanta, where she lives. She didn't know any of the organizers but decided to just show up wearing a T-shirt bearing Jordan's photo. There, she met organizers from several national gun control groups, and one of their leaders asked if she would be willing to speak to other mothers. Since then she has spoken to state legislators in Georgia and Florida, at the White House, and at numerous universities. She has done many television and radio interviews about Jordan's case, and she started the Walk with Jordan Scholarship Foundation to provide educational and charitable help to promising high school students.

In testimony before a subcommittee of the U.S. Senate Judiciary Committee, she said:

"My son was named for the river Jordan. In the Bible, that river symbolized the crossing to freedom. Its waters marked the final steps to liberation and offered up the holy stream that baptized Jesus. Its name seemed a fitting choice for a boy born at the end of the twentieth century—a time when black people in this country had finally come into their own.

Jordan was named for a change in the tide, a decision to try harder and do better. He was my only child. He was raised with love and learning and a clear understanding of right and wrong. I have been without Jordan now since Thanksgiving weekend 2012, without him last Christmas and on his birthday in February. I never got to take his prom picture or see him graduate from high school. I can tell you all about him—about his easy smile, his first girlfriend, and his plans to join the Marines. I can tell you how he loved his dad's gumbo. And how they both rooted for the New York Giants. But you can never really know my boy. Because an angry man owned a gun, kept it close at hand, and chose to demonstrate unbridled hatred one balmy evening for reasons I will never understand. These laws empowered his prejudiced beliefs and subsequent rage over my son's own life, his liberty and pursuit of happiness. There will be no sense made of any of it, unless I and the families of other victims speak out to assure this kind of predatory violence ends."

In 2014, Lucy became a full-time advocate for Everytown, handling outreach to communities of faith and minority communities. "One thing I recognized when I started out as a volunteer: there were not many people involved who looked like me, doing this work," she tells me. "I felt deeply that if we didn't diversify the movement and embrace communities of color, we wouldn't be successful. And a lot of people have been very concerned about the question of how Christians can be pro-life but pro-gun at the same time."

Lucy grew up in a political household. She was raised in Joliet, Illinois, about 40 miles south of Chicago. Her father was a dentist who served in the U.S. Army Dental Corps and as the president of the Illinois branch of the National Association for the Advancement of Colored People for over 20 years; he worked actively for the passage of the Civil Rights Act of 1964. Her mother was a registered nurse.

"I know those genes filtered right on through to me," Lucy says. "I used to say to Jordan, 'I think you're going to be a social activist.'" As for religion? She grew up in the Lutheran church, but wasn't very devout or involved. But soon after her marriage to her husband, Ron, in 1989, she had what she calls a life-altering born-again experience. "My husband was out of town and I was in an upstairs bedroom, and suddenly I felt a kind of reverent fear. Everything turned effervescent white, and I could hear everything, even sounds from the other side of the lake where we lived. I felt this presence in the room with me that drew me down on my knees." She found herself asking for forgiveness. Since that time, she has tried to "walk as a Christian, not perfectly, but I've given my life over to God, and it has allowed me to do what I've been able to do."

Lucy's outreach in the evangelical community brought her into an extraordinary friendship with Rob Schenck, a nationally known leader of the U.S. evangelical movement and president of the Christian outreach ministry Faith and Action. Rob is a high-profile conservative Christian political leader who had become increasingly uncomfortable with what he perceived as a contradiction between the movement's simultaneous pro-life and pro-gun positions. Rob and Lucy—a progressive Democrat with pro-choice views—came together to explore the spiritual aspects of these questions in a powerful documentary called *The Armor of Light*, which takes its name from Romans 13:12. ("The night is nearly over; the day is almost here. So let us put aside the deeds of darkness and put on the armor of light.") Their conversations prompted Rob to travel the country to talk with other evangelical leaders about gun violence and ask them to contemplate whether being pro-gun and being pro-life is compatible.

Lucy's work has taken her to other places she never thought she would go, including that turn in the spotlight at the 2016 Democratic National Convention and a press conference at the White House to speak on behalf of President Obama's My Brother's Keeper initiative. "I sit with the president, legislators, national civic leaders, clergy, everywhere the doors are open and people welcome me," she says. "I'm just Jordan's mama. All I know is what I've been given to do and I'm learning. I can only speak from my heart."

Telling the story was achingly difficult in the early days, Lucy says, but it's easier now. "I don't cry as often because I'm operating far less from an emotional standpoint now. This is work that has to be done—and I'll be doing it until they close the lid on my coffin. I cry more in my private moments now."

Lucy isn't sure that her work will lead to reduced gun violence in her lifetime, but accepts that. She feels blessed and grateful, even with the tragedy of Jordan's death. "I may never see the change," she says, "but I will live the rest of my life knowing that I did my best, and I've done what I'm supposed to do. It's like believing in God, even though I've never seen Him."

CHAPTER SIX

WHO IS MOST LIKELY TO EXPERIENCE POST-TRAUMATIC GROWTH (AND WHAT IF YOU DON'T)?

Trauma affects all of us at one point or another—it is part of the human experience. And researchers say that transformative growth after a jolt happens fairly often. But the phenomenon is hardly universal. Who is most likely to experience growth after trauma, and who isn't? And how can stories of transformation affect trauma survivors who don't experience growth?

"I Nearly Died. So What?"

That was the eye-catching headline on an essay by writer Meghan Daum about a severe case of typhus that nearly killed her in 2010. When she came out of a medically induced coma and recovered, religious friends wanted to know if the close call had caused her to think differently about her agnosticism. It hadn't. Secular friends were eager to hear about any spiritual or moral transformations she might have experienced. There weren't any. "Please don't misunderstand me," she wrote in her essay. "I was grateful to be alive, physically and cognitively—and, to be honest, even more grateful not to have emerged from the coma alive but with severe and irreparable brain damage. But I also knew myself well enough to suspect that after a few months of smelling the metaphorical flowers, I'd probably go back to being the whiny ingrate I was before."

Meghan isn't really all that whiny, but she did go back to the life she had before her devastating illness—and it was a pretty good life at that. An opinion columnist for the *Los Angeles Times*, Meghan also writes for *The New Yorker*, *The New York Times Magazine*, *The Atlantic*, and *Vogue*. She teaches writing at Columbia University's School of the Arts. She won a Guggenheim Fellowship in 2015 and a National Endowment for the Arts Fellowship in 2016. She is married and lives a comfortable life in New York City. In her writing, she draws unflinchingly from painful aspects of her own life, including troubled relationships with her mother and grandmother, her mother's death, and her decision not to have children. And, of course, the close call with her own death.

Trauma affects all of us at one point or another, but the phenomenon of post-traumatic growth is hardly universal.

And some clinicians worry that popularization of stories of growth can lead trauma victims to feel inadequate by comparison—or even feel a sense of failure or guilt.

Among researchers who study post-traumatic growth, there is no clear consensus on who is likely to experience the phenomenon and who is not—or why. Two leading researchers in the field, Lawrence Calhoun and Richard Tedeschi, have attempted to quantify and define the phenomenon by developing a tool for assessing and scoring it, called the Post-Traumatic Growth Inventory (PTGI). Trauma victims are asked to rate themselves on a numerical scale for 21 statements, organized around five factors: relating to others, new possibilities, personal strength, spiritual change, and appreciation of life.

Two possible predictors of post-traumatic growth are gender and age. Calhoun says that women are more likely to experience post-traumatic growth than men. "We think that telling others about your experience, and the response you get from others, is an important part of the growth process for some people," he says. "Men are less likely to engage in high levels of self-disclosure about their psychological processes than women. And women often are better equipped to respond when others disclose those things to them." He adds that this differential in experience of post-traumatic growth may have to do with a greater capacity among women to accept and assess accurately their own internal states.

In my interviews with trauma survivors, women have been quick to open up, sharing intimate details of their struggles to recover and the pain that has stayed with them years after trauma. Molly MacDonald, who lost everything she owned and endured breast cancer, revealed that she still feels the painful humiliation of standing outside a grocery store with $1.60 in her pocket to buy food for her children. Liz Alderman still aches audibly when she speaks about the hole in her life left by the death of her son, Peter, on 9/11. Marietta Jaeger's grief is never far from the surface when she talks about what her daughter, Susie, endured before she was murdered in 1973.

But many of the men I interviewed were comfortable sharing their emotions. I watched Bill Pelke cry openly in front of an audience of several hundred University of Houston students as he described his fight to save his grandmother's murderer, Paula Cooper, from the death penalty. Fifteen years after he nearly lost his life in an electrical fire,

Dave Schury wept openly when I asked him to describe details of his accident. Craig Corrie speaks candidly and freely of his psychological struggles after his daughter Rachel was crushed to death by an Israeli Defense Forces bulldozer.

There is no strong consensus among psychologists on the importance of gender as a predictor of post-traumatic growth. Dozens of research papers have examined the issue. One overview of the studies found varying results, noting that a 1996 study by Richard Tedeschi and Lawrence Calhoun found "significant gender difference in PTG" using the authors' Post-Traumatic Growth Inventory. The paper also noted that research has found gender differences across many different types of trauma, including cancer, HIV/AIDS, terrorism, and natural disasters. But other studies have found no significant gender difference in the likelihood of post-traumatic growth.

Age may be another predictor of growth. The review of post-traumatic growth research suggests that women over age 35 are more likely to report growth following trauma. The research in this area is tentative, but the impetus to think deeply about finding purpose in life is a dominant theme in organizations like Encore.org, which focuses on purposeful career reinvention for older people. "What I've noticed is how prevalent the jolt impetus is in our community," says Marc Freedman, Encore's founder. "We see it all the time—people who have been around long enough to see that life is finite, that there are a deeper set of issues than the ones that occupy our daily lives, and there is enough time to do something significant." Support from others may also be a critical factor of whether growth occurs—whether from therapists, friends, family members, or the broader social community. Eva Leivas-Andino found a community at the YES Institute that helped her come to terms with her conflicted emotions about her son's sexuality and her reaction to it. This community helped her transition to a new career working with teens on sexual identity and gender. Dave Schury began to see his path forward during his first visit to burn camp, where he was embraced by a community of other burn victims. Marietta Jaeger and Bill Pelke created a community of people traumatized by the loss of loved ones that has propelled them on their lifelong quest to end the death penalty. When Journey of Hope members meet each year, they are not only campaigning for political change—they are supporting one another. They listen to each other tell stories they have heard many times before. They bear witness and provide plenty of hugs. The trips are nurturing and rejuvenating.

Some researchers think that support from spouses can also be a key factor affecting growth. Research by psychologist Amy Canevello points in this direction for couples who experience a traumatic event together. The relationships of Cindy and Craig Corrie and Steve and Liz Alderman, who lost children in tragic circumstances, demonstrate the support couples can gain from each other. They play off each other's strengths and fill in each other's weaknesses.

Some jolt survivors may not experience growth, but they do exhibit resilience. That is, they bounce back and go on with their lives. Meghan Daum claims that she didn't grow following her near-death experience, but she did absorb the blow and return to her life as it was. Dennis S. Charney, an expert on the neurobiology and treatment of mood and anxiety disorders, writes that resilient people are able to cope with trauma—either they do not develop stress-related symptoms, or if they do, they are able to move ahead with their lives. "For a period after their ordeal, they may become distressed, but in time they will bounce back and carry on," he says. "For some, it will be almost as if the trauma had never occurred. For others, the distress will persist, but they will find healthy ways to cope."

Are there predictors of resilient responses in the aftermath of trauma? Charney and another researcher, Steven M. Southwick, tried to get at the question by studying three groups of people among whom they found high levels of resilience: former prisoners of war in Vietnam, Special Forces instructors, and civilians who have bounced back from traumatic events. They identified ten coping mechanisms that they call "resilience factors":

- Maintaining an optimistic but realistic outlook
- Facing fears
- Relying on an inner moral compass
- Turning to religious or spiritual practices
- Seeking and accepting social support
- Imitating sturdy role models
- Maintaining physical fitness
- Maintaining brain fitness
- Finding a way to accept things they cannot change
- Taking responsibility for their emotional well-being; many use their traumatic experience as a platform for personal growth

Can the expectation of growth place undue pressure on trauma victims? Calhoun worries that it can happen. "We don't want to create an expectation that growth should necessarily happen in all cases," he says. "It's not difficult to imagine people saying, 'Wow, I'm devastated and depressed—and you're telling me I'm inadequate because I'm not experiencing growth?'" In their clinical practice, Calhoun and Tedeschi follow a model of "expert companionship" that is careful to avoid pressing patients to expect growth from themselves. Here's how they describe the model in their book, "Post-Traumatic Growth in Clinical Practice"

"The term emphasizes the view that both professional expertise and human companionship are crucial for the people seeking our help. This stance can be crucial in facilitating the process of post-traumatic growth. We choose these words we use carefully; we see ourselves as *facilitators* rather than creators of growth, *companions* who offer some expertise in nurturing naturally occurring processes of healing and growth. Just as we can think of many of the procedures that physicians perform on the body as facilitating a healing process that the body must ultimately do for itself, we see ourselves as likewise facilitating a healing process that is psychological. In trauma survivors, the injuries are often so great that this process is too disturbed or challenged to function smoothly, so our job as professionals is to help it work more effectively."

Meghan Daum found the growth expectations suffocating—more so than the near-death experience she had managed to survive.

In the fall of 2010, Meghan was living in Los Angeles, and staying with a friend in Brooklyn when she was suddenly "hit with flu symptoms that felt like a truck had driven through the apartment and parked on my head," she says. "One minute I felt reasonably okay, if a little sniffly; the next minute I was shivering almost too violently to hold a cup of tea. Still, I assumed it was the flu, so did a doctor friend and the various pharmacists I consulted when I could drag myself out to the drugstore."

Three days later, back at home in Los Angeles after a tortuous plane ride, Meghan could barely walk. She was hospitalized, losing strength, and ultimately was placed in a medically induced coma while doctors worked to identify the cause of her illness: it was a bacterial infection, typhus, caused by flea bites. Among other complications, she had disseminated intravascular coagulation, a disorder in which the proteins that control blood clotting become overactive. Small blood clots form in the blood vessels, cutting off blood flow to organs such as the liver, brain, and kidneys. Doctors initially suspected a mosquito bite she got while staying with her friend in Brooklyn, but finally concluded that the disease came from feces carried by fleas on her friend's dog. They feared permanent brain damage—or that she wouldn't make it at all. But Meghan did recover, escaping with no more than tinnitus and some minor hearing loss.

"This will be reported to the county health department and someday I'll even record a 'survivor's testimony' video for a flea-borne typhus symposium at the Mosquito and Vector Control Association of California's annual meeting," she would write later in an essay about the experience. "In the meantime, the doctors will remain mystified by how I managed to get so sick from something that usually just gives people flu symptoms for a few days and then goes away. Moreover, they will be shocked at how quickly I got better. It will be as if grave illness were a deep swimming hole I plunged down to the bottom of and then shot back out of at the last possible second. They will tell me I scared them. A patient care coordinator who read my chart when I was in the ICU will come into my room and tell me that it is quite literally a *miracle* that I've recovered. The neurologist will also use the word *miracle*. This will give me chills. Neurologists shouldn't use words like *miracle*. Only evangelical Christians should. And even then they should choose their audiences wisely."

Then started the questions—what had Meghan learned from her near-death experience? "In one instance, a friend who is an Evangelical Christian told me that a lot of people had been praying for my recovery, and did it change my belief system?" she says. "I was so taken aback. It didn't make me a believer, but I didn't want to seem ungrateful for their prayers. That was the most extreme version of guilt—I felt that I was letting them down, and couldn't give them the answer they wanted. Some of this was the near-death experience. Was there a white light? The answer is no. I was just freaking out."

Lying in her hospital bed, Meghan even felt herself thinking that she ought to be able to change as a result of what she had gone through. She began to think that if she survived, she would make an effort to "behave more like an adult" in her relationships with her husband and her father. She even started to think about having a baby—something she had never really desired. But she knew it was just fantasy in her case.

"As I inch toward the shore, I am collecting the pieces of myself that were swept away with the tide but are floating back to me now," she wrote later in an essay. "I am reclaiming my words. I am locating the letters of the alphabet and arranging them so that they correspond with the ideas in my head. I am coming back to myself. And I am no wiser or more evolved than I was before. There is no epiphany or revelation or aha moment or big click. There is no redemption. There is no great lesson learned. There is only the unknowable and the unspeakable. There was only the unlikely if ever-present possibility that life is just a string of stories inside a coma. And in this story, I am not a better person.

I am the same person. This is the story with a happy ending. Or at least something close enough."

Meghan did become pregnant, but miscarried. And she says she has gone on as she was before, for the most part. The expectation that her near-death experience should have led to profound change in her life is a type of unwanted pressure, and it can lead people to feel like failures, she thinks. "There is a tyranny to epiphany," she told me in our interview. "This expectation that I'm going to change after this. It's a cultural demand that you see a lot in movies and in books. But sometimes, you don't become better or learn anything. We're obsessed with stories of triumph over adversity, but increasingly we're obsessed not just with victory but with redemption," she adds.

Kimina Lyall also worries about the pressures created by the hero mythology after trauma. On December 26, 2004, the Australian journalist was on a small island on the western coast of Thailand near the Indian Ocean when the third-largest earthquake in recorded history struck near the west coast of Sumatra in Indonesia. The resulting tsunami killed 230,000 people in 14 countries, overwhelming coastal communities in areas up to 100 feet high. In Thailand, more than 8,200 people died.

Kimina was the foreign correspondent for Southeast Asia for *The Australian* newspaper. She was based in Bangkok, but she and her partner, J.P., had built a vacation cottage on Golden Buddha Beach, a beautiful, barely inhabited resort island along the western coast on the Andaman Sea, which is part of the Indian Ocean. Known for ecotourism and popular with yoga aficionados, the island was reachable only by boat—and had no roads or electricity. The local economy was devoted mostly to fishing. When the tsunami approached that morning, Kimina was doing yoga when she heard a roar as loud as a jet passing overhead—so loud it stunned her. Running up to a small rise on top of the beach, she really did expect to see a fighter jet flying low over the water; instead, she saw what looked like a giant wave drawing water away from the shore. The first tsunami wave hit five minutes later—36 feet high and carrying a huge, destructive force. She managed to scramble up a small mountain before the waves hit. From there, she watched in disbelief and horror as the water quickly inundated the beaches and resort facilities.

"On Monkey Mountain, the water splashed over the lower ridge where many of the resort's frightened guests had retreated," she would write later. "But the waves' real impact came from their width. As the column of water flattened out over the shallower sea floor, the brown liquid formed a series of traveling steps, as broad as they were high, that packed on top of one another as they hit our beach, battering my friends with punch after punch of power.

"Within seconds, the water had washed over the trees, rushing up their trunks and submerging the lower branches, forming ugly rivers of debris-filled currents as it rocked back and forth from the bay to the beach, as if it were sloshing from side to side in a giant bathtub. Each of the people swirling around inside it was alone. Those rings of water, flowing from Sumatra to Thailand and, hours later, to Africa's east coast, connected hundreds of thousands of people to the world's largest natural disaster in living memory. But for those caught in its tumble, the experience was intensely private."

For Kimina, the chaos and stress that followed the tsunami were tangled up with other trauma. One was a sexual assault that she suffered early in her posting to Bangkok. The rape had occurred on a deserted beach, and her search for healing in some ways had led to her presence on the beach when the tsunami hit. In the wake of the tsunami, she worked hard to report on the disaster for her paper. Rather than take the time to care for herself and J.P., she rushed straight into covering the disaster—something she later came to see as a mistake that hurt their relationship and her own recovery from post-traumatic stress.

She also was struggling with a brewing career crisis. Nearing the end of her stint in Southeast Asia, Kimina was thinking of getting out of journalism altogether. As a foreign correspondent, she wrote later, she felt that she was "darting from one person's trauma to another's." She had "interviewed survivors of Pol Pot's murderous regime, picked through the remnants of vegetable markets decimated by homemade bombs, met child victims of predatory Australian 'sexpats,' and attended the press conference of Gracia Burnham, an American missionary who had spent a year being dragged in chains through the southern Philippines jungle as a hostage of a militant terrorist gang."

Kimina returned to the newsroom in Melbourne six months after the tsunami. She found that she could not let go of the sheer terror and trauma of what she had experienced in Thailand. "I remember covering the political response to a vague threat that some terrorist had made against Australia and standing at the back of a press conference being held by the premier and just rolling my eyes at the panicked response. I was saying to myself, 'You guys don't even know what it is like to live in a world where your life is in danger every single day and the threat isn't just terrorism—but actual terror, violence, insecurity, and instability.' I just couldn't reconcile those two worlds."

Kimina also struggled with survivor guilt. "I actually came out unscathed, compared with everything else I was witnessing around me. I knew people who lost their homes, their livelihoods, and dozens of members of their extended families, and the clothing on their backs.

For people who were tossed about by the waves, the force of the wave stripped them naked. They literally were starting from ground zero. And here I was—I still had my job, all of my income, and my assets. And I couldn't deal with the fact that I didn't have a right to be feeling what I was feeling."

The meaning and self-esteem Kimina had taken from her work in journalism were gone, but no new sense of mission had taken their place—she just felt traumatized and devastated. She left journalism, taking a senior executive position with a large Australian company that provides healthcare, financial services, and senior living services. Kimina has responsibility for strategy, corporate communications, and brand development. She likes the work—it is less stressful than the newsroom, and co-workers treat one another well. And she feels much more focused on the importance of human connection and relationships. "I like myself better now, I feel like I'm a gentler person. I'm more tolerant of other people—less judgmental, things are less black and white. And I think some of that came from the tsunami and the experiences afterward."

But the job isn't a new calling. She is studying psychology and has become an even more avid practitioner of yoga, but she still feels unsettled. "I don't have that kind of grand story to tell about how I'm going to dedicate my life to a purpose. I wouldn't say I feel lost, exactly, but I don't have a real clear direction on where to go from here."

And she worries that stories of heroic action in the face of trauma can create a sense of shame for those who don't experience the heroic rebound. "I think those stories are true—they do happen," she says. "But there is some mythology around trauma—and one element is the inner hero," she says. "There's the person who suddenly is able to lift the car off the child who is being squashed, or the person who stays on the plane until the last person gets off and finds this sort of previously unknown inner Hercules. Lots of people have those experiences, but I fear sometimes for those people who don't and what these stories mean to them. You have all the trauma but you don't have the redemption."

CHAPTER SEVEN

THE GIFT OF TRAUMA

Many jolt survivors regard their trauma as a gift of profound, valuable change. But what are the lessons the rest of us can learn from these stories of transformation? Do the experiences of trauma survivors teach us anything about how we can become more altruistic, empathetic, and appreciative of life? Can we learn anything about getting through our own life jolts, large and small?

I asked Hanh Meyers this question: "If you could wave a magic wand and return to your life as it was before the death of your husband, would you do it?"

She took a deep breath. "Obviously, I would want John here, but if he's not going to be here—no, I wouldn't trade. If I had a choice, I want him to be there to share my life, but his death and Liam's birth clarified for me what living is supposed to be about. You can't take each day for granted. There are days I wish I was naive again—thinking I would work at a law firm, we'd have a house in the suburbs, have all these kids and grow old together. But now, I wouldn't want to go back to that naive state."

Many jolt survivors feel this way—they regard their trauma as a gift of profound, valuable change. Those who have lost children or spouses, as Hanh did, would wave a magic wand to bring them back, of course. Yet even in the wake of her son Jordan's murder, Lucy McBath thinks of her new work as the best thing she has ever done. "I hate the way that I've come to the work," she says, "but it's what I was meant to do—it's where I'm gifted."

Would Molly MacDonald wave a wand to make her breast cancer and financial hardship disappear? "No," she tells me. "I lost everything I *thought* had value and found out what really does." Would Dave Sanderson wave a wand to not be on Flight 1549, which crash-landed in the Hudson River? "No, I truly believe I was supposed to be on that plane for a reason," he says. Would Kate Williams wave a wand to restore her eyesight? "No, absolutely not," she says. "What I found is that almost everything I've been up against, even though sometimes I get angry or frustrated, there is almost always a solution."

The essential "gift" of trauma is that it shakes everything up—our expectations for the future, our values, and how we want to spend our time. "Trauma is an intensifying experience," says journalist David Bornstein, who has interviewed many jolt survivors in his work writing about social innovation. "It becomes virtually impossible to pursue a normal course of action, the normal pleasures of life." Jolt survivors find themselves forced to reassess. They ask themselves difficult questions about their priorities, and then many take action that leads to profound, lasting change.

For some, the changes are internal and personal. The death of John Meyers sent Hanh on a painful inward-looking hunt for her own identity. A stroke prompted journalist Andrew Revkin to commit to his passion for music. When her eyesight began to fail, Kate Williams started writing, every day, in a diary the five things for which she was grateful: her work, the thrill of helping students realize goals, family, even public transportation that makes possible her independent life. She has kept up her journaling habit ever since.

Many jolt survivors are on a mission to create change in their communities or in the world. John Gallina and Dale Beatty recovered from traumatic injuries in Iraq and then returned home to build houses for homeless veterans. Liz and Steve Alderman created a network of mental health clinics in traumatized post-conflict societies after losing their son on 9/11. Cindy and Craig Corrie threw themselves into the cause of justice for Palestinians after their daughter was crushed by an Israeli bulldozer during a protest in Gaza. Marietta Jaeger devoted her life to the cause of ending the death penalty after the horrific murder of her young daughter at the hands of a serial killer.

What are the lessons for the rest of us? Do the experiences of trauma survivors teach us anything about how we can become more altruistic, empathetic, and appreciative of life? And can we learn anything about getting through our own life jolts, large and small?

One place to start is to recognize that trauma is a part of life for all of us. Fortunately, most of us will not suffer a dramatic traumatic event like a plane crash or terror attack or an electrical explosion. But we all suffer emotional crises, illnesses, the death of family members and friends. Many have experienced the financial and emotional trauma of lost work and income during the economic turmoil of the past decade. There are near-misses: a narrowly avoided auto accident, walking away from a cycling accident with no more than scrapes and bruises but knowing it could have been much worse. The sense of vulnerability we all feel in an age of mass shootings and terror attacks. The ongoing trauma of gun violence and young men who fall victim to police violence in the African-

American community. Trauma is part of the human condition, but it's all too easy to shut it out without taking the opportunity to reflect on its meaning. Is it possible to listen to your inner voice in a deeper way and make that voice so loud that the idea of continuing without making changes becomes intolerable?

Alice Graham did grab that opportunity. The jolt that changed her life took place in the wake of one of the worst disasters in American history: Hurricane Katrina. Although the hurricane didn't affect her directly, the jolt she experienced was a result of it. Alice had just arrived in Ocean Springs, a small city along Mississippi's Gulf Coast that had been ravaged by Katrina's 100-mile-per-hour winds and storm surge. She had seven students in tow from the North Carolina theological seminary where she was a professor; the group had come to volunteer in the disaster relief efforts. Alice was 62 years old, but in her mind, she was flashing back to another Mississippi tragedy: the brutal murder in 1955 of Emmett Till.

Back then, Alice was a nine-year-old African-American growing up in Chicago, just a few years younger than Till, who was abducted and brutally murdered in a tiny Mississippi town for allegedly flirting with a white woman. Till was from Chicago, and it was a defining moment for Alice. "It was a pivotal experience in the way I related to the South," she explains. "At that point, I made a commitment to myself that I would never go to Mississippi, because that was a dangerous place."

Fast-forward to 2005. Alice held a doctorate in pastoral psychology and was teaching at Hood Theological Seminary in Salisbury, North Carolina. She was enjoying a successful academic career and was just a few years away from retirement. But Alice was troubled by what was going on in Mississippi in the wake of the hurricane. A friend who was working on the Gulf Coast suggested that Alice bring some students down to volunteer, and she decided to offer a course that would include a 10-day trip to help the relief efforts. "I wanted them to experience the things about pastoral care that they would not get in a typical seminary curriculum," Alice tells me. "I thought Katrina was a really good chance for them to see what it means to minister in a crisis."

But en route to the Gulf Coast, old fears came flooding back. "We were driving down in the van, and I suddenly realized—I'm going to Mississippi! I was very anxious about it, because I was bringing black and white students."

On arrival, they stopped at an Ocean Springs restaurant that was filled with white patrons. The hostess, noticing the group's disaster relief identification tags, asked where they were from. "When we told her that we'd come down to volunteer and to see how we could be of help, she turned around and announced that to the entire restaurant. And the entire place applauded. So that kind of broke the myth that I had been living with."

"It's a moment where you're caught, and time stops. I realized that my mindset no longer was real," she says. "Here is a very welcoming community that was glad we were there."

The group's first assignment was at a grocery distribution center. "People would drive through in trucks, vans, and cars, and we'd have conversations to help us understand what kind of food packages to put together for them. It was middle-class and wealthy people in line with poor people, blacks in line with whites. The conversations we had were just amazing. I'm a certified pastoral counselor, and I didn't expect that depth of learning that I had.

"I'll never forget talking with one woman of deep faith who said, 'I've had everything I've wanted in my life; I've been able to go out and buy whatever I wanted. And here, I can't do anything. But I've got the lord.' It was those conversations that helped me move to a place of really loving these people."

Alice returned to the seminary, but felt that she was in the wrong place. Students noticed that she would frequently bring up examples in her teaching from Mississippi; they could see that she was excited about the work she'd done there.

"I needed to be in Mississippi," Alice says. "I felt like I had been reminded of why I had been called to the ministry." She began exploring ways to return to Mississippi as a teacher, but no spots were available. "That began a process of spiritual discernment, asking, 'What do you want me to do about it? What is the work?'"

Alice decided to roll the dice, giving up the security of her teaching position by taking early retirement at age 63. She moved to the Gulf Coast without a job lined up, but quickly was recruited to become executive director of Interfaith Partnerships, a nonprofit that works on disaster preparedness and poverty relief work. Later, she took the helm at another nonprofit group, Back Bay Mission, affiliated with the United Church of Christ, which supports residents of the Mississippi Gulf Coast with programs focused on education, emergency assistance, housing rehab, and homelessness prevention.

Katrina had shaken up Alice's life—she had not lived through the storm's devastation herself, but she was open to change, thoughtful about how to respond to what she was seeing and feeling around her. "I certainly never would have looked at moving to Mississippi under any circumstance. That just wasn't on my radar—and neither was running a grassroots community organization. What amazes me most is that I seem to do it well, and it is profoundly satisfying."

The transformation she experienced also has made her more comfortable with uncertainty and ambiguity—and more willing to take a risk. These days, she dreams of moving to Africa when she retires from Back Bay Mission. "Maybe Ghana, to do some work there. I don't know what exactly, but I know there will be something else. But one of the things this part of the journey tells me is to be comfortable with ambiguity."

Personal reflection of the kind Alice engaged in is an important starting point for anyone seeking change, writes life coach Richard Leider. "If you talk with people in the latter part of their lives and ask them to look back on how they've lived, you'll hear a consistent refrain: 'If I were to live my life over, I'd be more reflective.'"

Leider breaks down reflection into two parts: going higher and going deeper. "Higher" means looking up and around to consider what is causing stress and desire for change in your external environment. "Deeper, on the other hand, is when we go within," he writes. "We start to turn the questions inward. What are my choices? What are my real possibilities? When you turn inward, you begin to discover what's essential. It's when you learn what's core for you. Going inside gives you the chance to discover what doesn't change about you, no matter how much change is going on outside in the world. It gives you a chance to record the things in your life that are non-negotiable."

Trauma can also bring home the point that if you're going to make changes, you had better get on with it. And this is a point anyone can embrace with some effort—contemplating the reality of our own mortality also can help focus the mind on the possibility of change. (As the website *The Onion* put it in this satirical news headline: "World Death Rate Holding Steady At 100 Percent.")

Buddhist monks train to understand the transitory nature of life by staring at photos of decomposing bodies. "Theoretically, we know we will all die at some point, but we do our best to ignore the inevitability of death," writes the 17th Karmapa, Ogyen Trinley Dorje, the spiritual head of one of the major schools of Tibetan Buddhism. "The only way to escape death is to prevent birth, since everything that is born will eventually die. But preventing birth is utterly out of the question for us. Obviously, we have already been born. Since birth and death are natural pairs in this sense, we are bound to die. These can be very hard facts to face, I know. But denying them can cause us a great deal of pain. It can leave us emotionally vulnerable when things do come to an end, as they inevitably will. Uncomfortable as it may seem, accepting the facts of this reality puts us in a much better position to face major changes in our life wisely."

One practicing Buddhist who has considered this challenge deeply is David Kaczynski. If David's family name sounds familiar, it is with good reason: he is the brother of Ted Kaczynski, better known as "the Unabomber." Ted Kaczynski engaged in a 17-year nationwide bombing campaign against people involved with technology, planting and mailing homemade bombs. He ultimately killed three people and injured 23 others. David's trauma began in 1996 when he and his wife, Linda, became suspicious that Ted might be the bomber—suspicions that turned into certainty when *The New York Times* and *The Washington Post* both published a rambling manifesto written by the Unabomber in hopes that someone would recognize his writing and help track him down. David found himself forced to turn in his own brother; the pain and trauma of that decision and what followed sent him on his own spiritual journey of recovery and growth. Ted pled guilty in 1998 and was sentenced to life in prison with no chance of parole.

David and Linda had been practicing Buddhists for many years when the Unabomber crisis came to its conclusion. A social worker by training, David, at the time of Ted's arrest, was running a shelter for homeless runaway youth, many of whom had experienced severe traumas. His life has changed dramatically since then. David and Linda were involved in a successful fight to avoid a death penalty for Ted, and David has become an advocate against the death penalty, working with Journey of Hope and other advocates. He also has bravely confronted the suffering caused by his brother, meeting with and even befriending some of the Unabomber's victims.

"Life is traumatic, but we spend a lot of time defending ourselves against it," he says. "We all know we will die, we all lose loved ones. And if we open our eyes we are all living in the shadow of extinction and death. The world is endangered in so many ways, but the threats seem abstract."

Contemplating mortality naturally leads to an assessment of what you have contributed to the greater good—and what you want to leave behind. In his book *The Road to Character*, *New York Times* columnist David Brooks describes this as the difference between "resume virtues and the eulogy virtues":

> "The resume virtues are the ones you list on your resume, the skills that you bring to the job market and that contribute to external success. The eulogy virtues are deeper. They're the virtues that get talked about at your funeral, the ones that exist

at the core of your being—whether you are kind, brave, honest or faithful; what kind of relationships you formed.

Most of us would say that the eulogy virtues are more important than the resume virtues, but I confess that for long stretches of my life I've spent more time thinking about the latter than the former. Our education system is certainly oriented around the resume virtues more than the eulogy ones. Public conversation is, too—the self-help tips in magazines, the non-fiction bestsellers. Most of us have clearer strategies for how to achieve career success than we do for how to develop a profound character."

Many of the jolt survivors you have met in this book have left their "resume virtues" behind—a process that begins with a greatly enhanced capacity to feel for others and to take action to make change happen. This starts with a magnified sense of empathy—the ability to identify and feel for others. As Bornstein puts it, jolt survivors have become "radically empathetic" to the point where they can identify with people very different from themselves. But many jolt survivors go far beyond empathy. Their stories hinge on compassion, which is empathy in action. They have found a new purpose in their lives that is life-saving—first for themselves, and then for others.

"It was the work that saved my life," as Liz Alderman said of the crisis she faced after her son's death in the World Trade Center on 9/11. "It gave me a reason to get out of bed, a reason to function at a high level and learn new things—get my brain working on something other than my loss. I thought I would never feel good about anything in my life again."

Lucy McBath says she has no idea what she would be doing if she had not been able to channel her pain and grief over Jordan's murder into her work on gun violence prevention. "It's kept me going full speed ahead—I'm just immersed in the work, and it gives me a way to make sense of what happened. The pain doesn't go away, and you don't want it to go away, because it keeps you grounded. But it's been very cathartic to move in a direction that could make a difference, so that this doesn't happen to anyone else. This is what I'll be doing until they lower me into the ground."

The discovery of purpose and meaning is transformative for many jolt survivors, but is it possible to develop a greater sense of empathy and compassion without suffering a trauma?

Psychologist Dacher Keltner argues that humans actually are hardwired through evolution to be compassionate, and that instincts toward compassion can be cultivated. In his research, Keltner has measured activity of a part of the human nervous system—the vagus nerve—that has been shown to be linked with emotions of empathy and compassion, and of the left frontal lobes of the brain, which support compassion-related feelings. He has found that practices such as mindfulness meditation, prayer, and yoga can dramatically increase the brain's capacity for compassion. So can simply contemplating suffering—brief exposure to images of people being harmed triggered activity of the vagus nerve.

Outside the realm of biological or psychological theory, faith or spiritual practice often serves as a bridge to compassion for jolt survivors. Consider the powerful urge felt by Marietta Jaeger to forgive her daughter's killer, driven by her deeply held Christian faith. That act of forgiveness allowed Marietta to free herself of the anger that was consuming her and to move on with her life, but it also opened the door for Marietta to empathize with a serial killer, to become more compassionate, and to devote the rest of her life to speaking out against the death penalty, attending annual fasting vigils on the steps of the U.S. Supreme Court, and visiting death row inmates well into her late 70s.

Back in 2008, a survey by the AARP found that just 20 percent of older Americans believe they will leave the world in better condition than they found it. At that time, the developed world was mired in the worst recession since the Great Depression, and reasons for pessimism might seem even more justified today. Problems such as global warming, terrorism, poverty, race relations, and gun violence seem insurmountable. Despite the pessimism in some quarters, more than 25 million Americans ages 50 to 70 years old are committed to putting their energies to work in careers that address social needs, according to a study by Encore.org, and about 4.5 million already are doing so. Those numbers express the human desire for purpose, to transcend one's own life to be part of something bigger. And as Victor Frankl observed, traumatic suffering isn't required for the discovery of purpose—it is possible to choose one's attitude. The stories of jolt survivors prove that it's not only possible but more fulfilling to live with purpose and intent. Purpose provides energy and focus and marries values with the way we live our lives. Most important, it answers our most profound questions about the legacy we will leave behind.

Our time is finite, our lives "wild and precious," as Mary Oliver reminds us. What will you do with yours?

THE WORK OF JOLT SURVIVORS

M any jolt survivors are engaged in the important work of social justice, serving others and making change happen in the world.

Liz and Steve Alderman

The Peter C. Alderman Foundation works to improve the quality of life of survivors, create healthier, peaceful populations, and influence the political will to put mental health on the global health agenda.
http://www.petercaldermanfoundation.org/

Cindy and Craig Corrie

The Rachel Corrie Foundation for Peace and Justice promotes human rights and social, economic, and environmental justice, with a specific focus on the Israel-Palestine conflict.
http://rachelcorriefoundation.org/

Dale Beatty and John Gallina

Purple Heart Homes provides housing assistance to veterans.
https://purplehearthomesusa.org/

Alice Graham

Back Bay Mission supports residents of the Mississippi Gulf Coast with programs focused on education, emergency assistance, housing rehab, and homelessness prevention.
https://thebackbaymission.org/

Eva Leivas-Andino

The YES Institute provides community dialog and education on sexual orientation and youth suicide prevention in Florida and other states.
http://yesinstitute.org/

Molly MacDonald
The Pink Fund helps low-income women cope with the financial stress that can accompany a breast cancer diagnosis.
https://www.pinkfund.org/

Lucy McBath
Everytown for Gun Safety is a national organization fighting to reduce gun violence.
https://everytown.org/

Mark Noonan
Elders in Action is a nonprofit advocacy group that assists seniors in the Portland, Oregon, area with housing, health, and elder abuse problems.
http://eldersinaction.org/

Bill Pelke and Marietta Jaeger
Journey of Hope, an organization led by murder victims' family members, conducts public education speaking tours and addresses alternatives to the death penalty.
https://www.journeyofhope.org/

Dave Schury
From Tragedy to Triumph Foundation raises funds to award college scholarships to burn survivors.
http://www.ftttf.org/

Kate Williams
LightHouse for the Blind and Visually Impaired offers services for the visually challenged that help promote equality and self-reliance.
http://lighthouse-sf.org/

FURTHER READING

These books, articles, and documentaries provided inspiration and guidance for this book.

Psychology and Psychiatry

Post-Traumatic Growth in Clinical Practice, by Lawrence G. Calhoun and Richard G. Tedeschi. This book by two important pioneers in researching post-traumatic growth is written for clinicians, but in clear language that laypeople can understand. Calhoun and Tedeschi describe their clinical experiences working with patients who have experienced post-traumatic growth. (Routledge, 2013).

Resilience: The Science of Mastering Life's Greatest Challenges, by Steven M. Southwick and Dennis S. Charney. An investigation of ways people bounce back from stress and trauma. Offers a useful point of comparison to the study of post-traumatic growth. (Cambridge University Press, 2012).

Positivity: Top-Notch Research Reveals the Upward Spiral That Will Change Your Life, by Barbara Fredrickson. An exploration of how positive emotions promote healing and change. (Harmony, 2009)

Trauma and Recovery: The Aftermath of Violence—From Domestic Abuse to Political Terror, by Judith Herman, M.D. Drawing on her research on domestic violence, Dr. Herman explores connections between private traumas, such as rape and domestic violence, to public traumas, such as terrorism and natural disasters. (Basic Books, 1992)

Personal Narratives

Lucy McBath

3½ Minutes, 10 Bullets. A documentary based on the events surrounding the 2012 shooting of Lucy's son, Jordan Russell Davis.
http://bit.ly/2fq9GTp

The Armor of Light. A documentary that explores the development of Lucy's extraordinary relationship with evangelical minister Richard Schenck. It investigates the question, is it possible to be both pro-gun and pro-life?
http://bit.ly/1LIs7Lk

Rachel Corrie

Let Me Stand Alone: The Journals of Rachel Corrie. A posthumous collection of Rachel Corrie's journal entries, letters, and drawings, selected by her family. (W. W. Norton & Company, 2009)

Rachel. An investigative documentary film by Simone Bitton that examines the circumstances of Rachel Corrie's death.
http://www.wmm.com/filmcatalog/pages/c787.shtml

Meghan Daum

The Unspeakable: And Other Subjects of Discussion. A collection of 10 essays by Meghan Daum, including "Diary of a Coma," in which she reflects on her near-death experience. (Picador, 2014)

David Kaczynski

Every Last Tie: The Story of the Unabomber and His Family. This is a personal memoir of the Kaczynski family's life together, coupled with David's ideas about reconciliation. (Duke University Press Books, 2016)

Kimina Lyall

Out of the Blue: Facing the Tsunami. Kimina Lyall's memoir of life on a small coastal island in Thailand before, during, and after the earthquake and tsunami in 2004. (ABC Books, 2006)

Bill Pelke

Journey of Hope: From Violence to Healing. Bill tells the story of his grandmother's death and his journey of forgiveness. With a foreword by Sister Helen Prejean. (Xlibris Corporation, 2003)

Andrew Revkin

"My Stroke of Luck." *The New York Times*, May 13, 2013. Andrew reflects in this blog post 22 months after his stroke.
http://nyti.ms/1GMoBKV

Spirituality and Purpose

The Road to Character, by David Brooks. *The New York Times* columnist challenges himself and his readers to rebalance between "resume virtues" and "eulogy virtues." (Random House, 2015)

Man's Search for Meaning, by Viktor E. Frankl. The Viennese psychologist invented an approach to psychotherapy centered on helping patients discover meaning in their lives. This seminal 1946 book begins with a memoir of the horrors Frankl endured in the Nazi death camps, and his path to discovering the importance of having a purpose in life. (Beacon Press, 2006)

The Heart Is Noble: Changing the World From the Inside Out, by the Karmapa, Ogyen Trinley Dorje. An emerging leader of Tibetan Buddhism offers thoughts on how to live with integrity in the modern world. (Shambhala, 2014)

The Power of Purpose: Find Meaning, Live Longer, Better, by Richard J. Leider. A well-known personal coach offers thoughts on how to unlock a sense of purpose. (Berrett-Koehler Publishers, 2015)

Social Justice

Change of Heart: Justice, Mercy, and Making Peace with My Sister's Killer, by Jeanne Bishop. The author narrates her transformative journey after the murders of her sister and brother-in-law. (Westminster John Knox Press, 2015)

How to Change the World: Social Entrepreneurs and the Power of New Ideas, by David Bornstein. How one person can make an astonishing difference in the world, explored through profiles of social entrepreneurs. (Oxford University Press, 2007)

The Big Shift: Navigating the New Stage Beyond Midlife, by Marc Freedman. The founder of the Encore career movement explains how to transform a midlife crisis into a midlife opportunity. (PublicAffairs, 2012)

A Path Appears: Transforming Lives, Creating Opportunity, by Nicholas Kristof and Sheryl WuDunn. Explores how altruism affects us, the markers for success, and how to avoid the pitfalls. (Knopf Doubleday Publishing Group, 2015)

CHAPTER NOTES

Epigraph

"The Summer Day" from *House of Light* by Mary Oliver, Published by Beacon Press Boston. Copyright © 1990 by Mary Oliver. Reprinted by permission of The Charlotte Sheedy Literary Agency Inc.

Introduction

In *The Hero With a Thousand Faces* by Joseph Campbell (Princeton University Press, 1969), mythologist Joseph Campbell traces the narrative of redemption through suffering in Christianity, Judaism, and Islam. He calls this the "monomyth" of the Hero's Journey.

For an understanding of the psychological research on post-traumatic growth, I have relied throughout this book on the work of Lawrence G. Calhoun and Richard G. Tedeschi, who are pioneers in the field, and especially on their book *Post-Traumatic Growth in Clinical Practice* (Routledge, 2013).

There is no strong consensus among psychologists on the importance of gender as a predictor of post-traumatic growth. See "Gender Differences in Self-Reported Post-traumatic Growth: A Meta-Analysis," by Tanya Vishnevsky, Arnie Cann, Lawrence G. Calhoun, Richard G. Tedeschi, and George J. Demakis. *Psychology of Women Quarterly* 34 (2010), pp. 110–120.

The connection between trauma and the search for meaning has roots in the work of psychologist and Holocaust survivor Viktor E. Frankl. See *Man's Search for Meaning* (Beacon Press, 2006).

Chapter One: Stronger, Fearless, and Vulnerable

Some details about the abduction and murder of Susie Jaeger are drawn from *Matador of Murder: An FBI Agent's Journey in Understanding the Criminal Mind*, by Patrick J. Mullany (CreateSpace Independent Publishing Platform 2015).

Marietta Jaeger wrote about Susie's murder in her book *The Lost Child* (Zondervan Publishing).

Statistics on the likelihood of suicide among lesbian, gay, and bisexual youth are drawn from "Suicide Risk and Prevention for Lesbian, Gay, Bisexual, and Transgender Youth," published in 2008 by the Suicide Prevention Resource Center Education Development Center.

The discussion of the issues that sightless people face in the workplace is informed by "Employer Attitudes Toward Blind or Visually Impaired Employees: Initial Development of a Measurement Instrument," by Michele Capella McDonnall. *Rehabilitation Counseling Bulletin* 58, no. 1 (2014): pp. 29–36.

Chapter Two: A Radical Sense of Empathy

Two books provided important background on the interwoven roles of trauma and purpose:

The Power of Purpose: Find Meaning, Live Longer, Better, 3rd ed. by Richard Leider (Berrett-Koehler Publishers, 2015).

Trauma and Recovery: The Aftermath of Violence—From Domestic Abuse to Political Terror, by Judith Herman (Basic Books, 1992).

Molly MacDonald

Data on how financial shocks affect American families was drawn from "How Do Families Cope with Financial Shocks?" Pew Charitable Trusts report, October 2015. http://www.pewtrusts.org/en/research-and-analysis/issue-briefs/2015/10/the-role-of-emergency-savings-in-family-financial-security-how-do-families

John Gallina and Dale Beatty

The discussion of post-traumatic growth in combat veterans was informed by the following research papers:

"Invisible Wounds of War: Psychological and Cognitive Injuries, Their Consequences, and Services to Assist Recovery," edited by T. Tanielian and Lisa H. Jaycox (Santa Monica, California: RAND Corporation, 2008).

"Epidemiology of PTSD," by Jaimie L. Gradus, DSc, MPH. U.S. Department of Veterans Affairs website. http://www.ptsd.va.gov/professional/PTSD-overview/epidemiological-facts-ptsd.asp

"Can We Facilitate Posttraumatic Growth in Combat Veterans?" by Richard G. Tedeschi and Richard J. McNally. *American Psychologist*, January 2011.

For information on the problem of homelessness among veterans, I relied on *The 2015 Annual Homeless Assessment Report to Congress*, by the U.S. Department of Housing and Urban Development Office of Community Planning and Development. https://www.hudexchange.info/resources/documents/2015-AHAR-Part-1.pdf

Cindy and Craig Corrie

Background on the death of Rachel Corrie came from these sources:

"Statement From the Parents of Rachel Corrie." The Electronic Intifada website, March 19, 2003. https://electronicintifada.net/content/statement-parents-rachel-corrie/210

International Solidarity Movement website. http://palsolidarity.org/about/faq/

"American Peace Activist Killed by Army Bulldozer in Rafah." *Haaretz* website, March 17, 2003. http://www.haaretz.com/american-peace-activist-killed-by-army-bulldozer-in-rafah-1.16010

"The Death of Rachel Corrie," by Joshua Hammer. *Mother Jones* website, September/October 2003. http://www.motherjones.com/politics/2003/09/death-rachel-corrie

"Rachel Corrie's Echo," by John Nichols. *The Nation* website, March 20, 2003. http://www.thenation.com/article/rachel-corries-echo/

"U.S.: Israeli Probe Into Rachel Corrie's Death Wasn't Credible," by Amira Hass. *Haaretz* website, August 23, 2012. http://www.haaretz.

com/israel-news/u-s-israeli-probe-into-rachel-corrie-s-death-wasn-t-credible-1.460091

Liz and Steve Alderman

For information on the scope of the mental health problem in less developed countries, I relied on "The Importance of Global Mental Health for the Sustainable Development Goals," by Nicole Votruba, Julian Eaton, Martin Prince, and Graham Thornicroft. *Journal of Mental Health* 23, no. 6 (2014).

For discussing the survival rates of nonprofit organizations, Thomas Pollack of the Center on Nonprofits and Philanthropy at the Urban Institute prepared an analysis of IRS data at my request.

Chapter Three: New Priorities
Andrew Revkin

Background on trends in strokes was drawn from *Heart and Stroke Statistics, 2016 Statistical Update* by the American Heart Association. https://www.heart.org/HEARTORG/General/Heart-and-Stroke-Association-Statistics_UCM_319064_SubHomePage.jsp

Two articles by Andrew Revkin are quoted:

"My Stroke of Luck." *The New York Times*, May 13, 2013. http://nyti.ms/1GMoBKV

"My Climate Change." *Issues in Science and Technology* XXXII, no. 2 (Winter 2016). http://issues.org/32-2/my-climate-change/

Hanh Meyers

Data on glioblastoma came from the American Brain Tumor Association website. http://www.abta.org/brain-tumor-information/types-of-tumors/glioblastoma.html

Chapter Four: The Process of Change

Background on the importance of interaction and support from family members and peers was drawn from an article by Lawrence G. Calhoun and Richard G. Tedeschi in a volume of essays they edited, *The Handbook of Posttraumatic Growth: Research and Practice* (Routledge, 2006), p. 12.

The discussion of how romantic partners can affect one another's recovery and growth relied on research by psychologist Amy Canevello and colleagues, especially the paper "Supporting Close Others' Growth After Trauma: The Role of Responsiveness in Romantic Partners' Mutual Posttraumatic Growth," by A. Canavello, V. Michels, and N. Hilaire. *Psychological Trauma: Theory, Research, Practice, and Policy*, September 21, 2015. http://dx.doi.org/10.1037/tra0000084

Frank Smyth

The description of Frank Smyth's experience in captivity during the Gulf War draws in part from his essay, "Tragedy in Iraq: One Journalist Died Covering the War in the Persian Gulf, Photographer Gad Gross. This Is the Story of How It Happened." *The Village Voice*, May 14, 1991. http://www.franksmyth.com/the-village-voice/tragedy-in-iraq/

Chapter Five: The Role of Faith and Spirituality

Background was drawn from "Spirituality and Trauma: An Essay," by Robert Grant, Ph.D. *Traumatology* 5, no. 1, March 1999.

Bill Pelke

Bill Pelke's 2003 book, *Journey of Hope: From Violence to Healing*, describes his journey through the tragedy that befell his family with the murder of his grandmother, and how he became an internationally known advocate for abolishing the death penalty. Along with my extensive interviews with Bill, this chapter draws on several passages in his book.

Lucy McBath

Background on Michael Dunn, the convicted killer of Jordan Davis, was drawn from the article "Michael Dunn: The Murderous Bullying S.O.B. That the Jury Hardly Knew," by Frank Vyan Walton. *The Daily Kos*, February 16, 2014. http://www.dailykos.com/story/2014/2/16/1277981/-Michael-Dunn-the-Murderous-Bullying-S-O-B-that-the-Jury-Hardly-Knew

Three articles informed the discussion of Stand Your Ground laws and their disparate racial impact:

"Killed by a Gun," by Marian Wright Edelman. *The Huffington Post* website, February 21, 2014. http://www.huffingtonpost.com/marian-wright-edelman/killed-by-a-gun_b_4834108.html

"More Homicides Are Reported in States Where You Can 'Stand Your Ground,' Report Finds," by Sarah Ferris. *The Washington Post* website, August 15, 2014. https://www.washingtonpost.com/blogs/govbeat/wp/2014/08/15/more-homicides-are-reported-in-states-where-you-can-stand-your-ground-report-finds/

"Do Stand Your Ground Laws Worsen Racial Disparities?" by J. Roman. The Urban Institute website, August 8, 2012. http://blog.metrotrends.org/2012/08/stand-ground-laws-worsen-racial-disparities/

Background on Mothers of the Movement, a group of African-American women who supported Hillary Clinton's 2016 White House bid, came from the article "Mothers of Black Victims Emerge as a Force for Hillary Clinton," by Amy Chozick. *The New York Times* website, April 13, 2016. http://www.nytimes.com/2016/04/14/us/politics/hillary-clinton-mothers.html Retrieved July 11, 2016

I also relied on the testimony of Lucy McBath before the Senate Judiciary Committee, Subcommittee on the Constitution, Civil Rights and Human Rights in *'Stand Your Ground' Laws: Civil Rights and Public Safety Implications of the Expanded Use of Deadly Force*, October 29, 2013.

An extraordinary documentary depicts the unlikely friendship that developed between Lucy McBath and a conservative evangelical minister. See "The Armor of Light and Inflaming the Conscience: A Conversation with Abigail Disney and Rob Schenck," by Alissa Wilkinson. *Christianity Today*, October 23, 2015. http://www.christianitytoday.com/ct/2015/october-web-only/armor-of-light-interview-abigail-disney-rob-schenck.html

Chapter Six: Who Is Most Likely to Experience Post-Traumatic Growth (and What if You Don't)?

The analysis of the contrast between resilience and growth was drawn from *Resilience: The Science of Mastering Life's Greatest Challenges*, by Steven M. Southwick, M.D. and Dennis S. Charney, M.D. (Cambridge University Press, 2012).

Lawrence G. Calhoun and Richard G. Tedeschi describe the role of expertise and help that professionals can provide in *Post-Traumatic Growth in Clinical Practice* (Routledge, 2013).

Meghan Daum

Background on Meghan's life-threatening illness was drawn from my interviews with her and two of her writings:

"I Nearly Died. So What?" *The New York Times*, November 14, 2014. http://www.nytimes.com/2014/11/16/opinion/sunday/i-nearly-died-so-what.html?_r=0

The Unspeakable and Other Subjects of Discussion. A collection of ten essays, including "Diary of a Coma," which reflects on her near-death experience. (Picador, 2014).

Kimina Lyall

Kimina's book *Out of the Blue: Facing the Tsunami* (ABC Books, 2006) offers a harrowing account of living through the third-largest earthquake in recorded history.

Chapter Seven: The Gift of Trauma

Richard Leider's comments on the importance of reflection were drawn from *Life Reimagined: Discovering Your New Life Possibilities*, by Richard J. Leider and Alan M. Webber (Berrett-Koehler Publishers, 2013).

The discussion of the inevitability of death, meditation on death, and how to think about legacy was drawn from these sources:

"World Death Rate Holding Steady at 100 Percent." *The Onion* website, January 22, 1997. http://www.theonion.com/article/world-death-rate-holding-steady-at-100-percent-1670.

The Heart Is Noble: Changing the World From the Inside Out, by the Karmapa, Ogyen Trinley Dorje (Shambhala, 2014).

The Road to Character, by David Brooks (Random House, 2015).

"More to Give: Tapping the Talents of the Baby Boomer, Silent and Greatest Generations," by John M. Bridgeland, Robert D. Putnam, and Harris L. Wofford (AARP, 2008). http://assets.aarp.org/rgcenter/general/moretogive.pdf

The discussion regarding psychologist Dacher Keltner on human compassion and evolution was drawn from his book *Born to Be Good: The Science of a Meaningful Life* (W.W. Norton, 2009).

The hunger for a second career with purpose is documented in the report "Encore Careers: The Persistence of Purpose." Encore.org, wesbite, 2014. http://encore.org/wp-content/uploads/files/2014Enco reResearchOverview.pdf

ACKNOWLEDGEMENTS

I began work on this book while I was doing something else. I have interviewed dozens of people as part of my work as a journalist covering retirement who were launching new careers, businesses, or nonprofit organizations. Very often, they were making changes to satisfy a desire for greater purpose and meaning in their lives, and over the years, I noticed a pattern: many had started down new life paths following a traumatic life experience. That observation led me to investigate the phenomenon further. I widened my lens beyond older Americans, listening to many more stories of transformation.

Often, I met people pursuing these new life paths at the annual conference organized by Encore, a nonprofit dedicated to purpose-driven second acts. Marc Freedman, Encore's founder and CEO, provided spiritual inspiration and has encouraged and supported my work on trauma and transformation every step of the way; Marci Alboher, an Encore vice president, connected me with several of the amazing people you will meet in the book.

AARP The Magazine published the feature article "Surviving the Jolt" in 2014, which preceded this book. David Dudley, who edited that article, helped shaped my thinking on trauma and transformation and pointed me toward important stories and resources. Jodi Lipson of AARP's book division also provided encouragement and insight on the structure and framing of the book.

Lawrence G. Calhoun, a pioneering researcher in post-traumatic growth, generously—and patiently—explained his work in our interviews. Numerous books and research papers by Calhoun and his colleague Richard Tedeschi also were important resources. Amy Canevello, a colleague of Calhoun's and Tedeschi's at the University of North Carolina Charlotte, provided insights on how post-traumatic growth can impact couples.

Thomas Pollack of the Center on Nonprofits and Philanthropy at the Urban Institute was kind enough to prepare an analysis of Internal Revenue Service data on the survival rate of nonprofit organizations.

Several colleagues and friends made important introductions to people you will meet in this book. They include Margaret Moses of Loyola University Chicago School of Law, who introduced me to her student Hanh Meyers, and Richard Eisenberg, who published a feature article about Amanda North on the website he edits, www.nextavenue. org. Lynn Pollack provided an introduction to Cindy and Craig Corrie. Bruce Shapiro of the Dart Center for Journalism & Trauma at Columbia University introduced me to Kimina Lyall. Psychotherapist Mark Brayne, former director of Dart's London center, provided valuable insight on how trauma impacts the lives of couples.

Early chapter readers included journalist Chris Farrell of American Public Media and leadership educator Mark Walton. My friends Leslie Nickels and Lon Berkeley opened the door to their longstanding book group, whose members read early chapters and provided helpful feedback. Author and career expert Kerry Hannon read early chapters, and served as a mentor throughout on the twists and turns of the publishing world.

Many friends—too numerous to name here—inquired often about my progress, opened up about their own experiences with trauma, and promised to read the finished book, no matter when I finished.

Anita Weinberg, the love of my life, read every word of this book with energy and enthusiasm, in many cases more than once. She asked perceptive questions, polished my prose, and challenged my thinking. She also helped to get me going when my energy flagged. Our children—Shira, Beth, and Asher—also read early chapters and were great supporters of their father along the way.

When I began work on this book, I worried that it would be difficult to convince people who had suffered severe trauma to agree to be interviewed. But most of the people I approached were eager to talk about their experiences, the lessons they have learned and the gift of transformation. The wonderful people who inhabit this book were very generous in sharing their stories. Searing pain has given them clarity about how they want to use their remaining time, and an inspiring strength of spirit that I will never forget. To them, I dedicate this book.

ABOUT THE AUTHOR

For more than a decade, Mark Miller has researched and written about what motivates people to reinvent their lives. He is also a nationally recognized expert on retirement and aging. He is a columnist for Reuters and other news outlets, and a contributor to *The New York Times*. Miller is the author of *The Hard Times Guide to Retirement Security*.